peace

TUCKER SHAW

AlloyBooks

For Geoffrey Shaw, who inspires peace.
And for everyone, everywhere,
who gives peace a chance.

Many, many thanks to the following:

Susan Kaplow, Stephanie Lane, Eloise Flood, Les Morgenstein, Josh Bank, Bobbie Gottschalk, John Wallach, Askari Mohammed, Luiz deBarros, Ken Legins, Billy Hallowell, Sarah Buchanan, Brett Adam, Janet Shaw, Deb Goldstein, Jin Moon, Saryn Chorney, Stephen Kolb, Mark Webber, Orlando Holguin, Bob Bell, Tasha Stoute, Terry Wang, Kirsten Hagon, Cherrie Welch, Laura Dower, Shan Jayakumar, Mike Fitzgerald.

Many thanks to Eve and Gwen Stefani for sharing their time and words.

This book could not have happened without the amazing energy and love of every single person mentioned in this book. To all of you who answered all my questions, from Indonesia to South Africa to Detroit to Ground Zero, thank you.

Onward, to peace!

ALLOY BOOKS
Published by the Penguin Group
Penguin Putnam Books for Young Readers,
345 Hudson Street, New York, New York 10014, U.S.A.

Published by Puffin Books,
a division of Penguin Putnam Books for Young Readers, 2002

10 9 8 7 6 5 4 3 2 1

Illustrations by Mike Reddy
Cover design by Marci Senders
Interior design by Jennifer Blanc

Produced by 17th Street Productions,
an Alloy, Inc. company
151 West 26th Street
New York, NY 10001

ISBN 0-14-230221-X
Printed in the United States of America

contents

Introduction

PEACE.

It's been quite a world since September 11, 2001. I'm sure we could use a little peace right now. Actually, we all could use a lot of peace right now. Make that forever.

Not too long ago, for most of us in the United States, peace was little more than a word. The idea of peace made us feel secure, or hopeful, or serene, but we didn't really understand it. It was a notion that we never really got a handle on, a concept that we could never entirely grasp, something we'd use as a greeting, even.

But for most of us, it was something we never really thought too hard about. Peace was like air, something we took for granted—until that September day when it was taken away.

Since then, things have changed. We now have new priorities, new challenges, new questions, new knowledge, new fears, new concerns, new heroes. We are, around the world, new people.

Peace really means something now. And it's something we are all responsible for. Each one of us. Working toward peace is within our control.

Sure, we don't get to control when our nation will go to war, and we can't predict when we might face another attack. But the individual decision to pursue a peaceful life is a choice we each get to make. Random acts of kindness around the neighborhood won't end war and conflict around the world, but they can make our own lives a bit more peaceful. And millions and millions of acts of kindness, strung together, can move us toward a more peaceful world over time.

I know, and you know, that it's not always a breeze to make the choice of peace. With everything going on in our personal lives and everything going on in the world, we often feel powerless when it comes to peace, whether it's the serenity of inner peace or the promise of world peace. The truth is, though, we're all equally powerful when it comes to creating and maintaining peace for ourselves.

We know now, after 2001, that the road to peace will always be a rough one . . . but the best we can do is to keep pushing in that direction, to keep working for peace.

That's why I created this book. When the journey to peace seems too long, too tough, or when violence, intolerance, and hate seem to gain the upper hand, turn to this book. It'll inspire you to take the high road, to choose kindness, respect, and peace.

It's got ideas and comments from many of you, first-person experiences in the struggle for peace, points of view from young people around the world, smart things that celebrities have said and done, and some song lyrics that really mean something.

Stick this book on your night table. Carry it with you in your backpack. Show it to your friends. Take the words in this book into the world and remind others about the hope of peace.

—*Tucker*

Because peace belongs to everyone on the planet, and because we want everyone to hear us, we figured we'd shout out in some different languages.

Throughout this book you'll find different ways of saying "peace" in languages from all around the world.

— SPANISH, PORTUGUESE, GALICIAN

"You always hear all these clichés about children and young people being the future. But that's not right. Young people are the now. We are the present."

—ANA, 17
THE PHILIPPINES

Part One

What is peace?

peace (*pēs*) *n.*
1. The absence of war or other hostilities. 2. An agreement or a treaty to end hostilities. 3. Freedom from quarrels and disagreement; harmonious relations. 4. Public security and order. 5. Inner contentment; serenity.

Interj. Used as a greeting or farewell, and as a request for silence.

— *The American Heritage Dictionary*, Fourth Edition

平和

—JAPANESE

Defining Peace

WHAT A CONCEPT, PEACE.

It means something different to everyone. For some of us, peace is about contentment and serenity on the inside. For others, it's being able to hit the streets without wondering whether we'll get home safely or whether someone we love will be killed or injured in that day's fighting. For some of us, peace is an end to a personal struggle. For some, it's achieving a goal. For others, it's an end to violence or abuse. Sometimes peace is about freedom from pain or fear. Sometimes it's about freedom in general.

Sometimes peace is personal. Sometimes it's political. Sometimes it's both.

On one hand, peace can be as simple as a sibling-free Saturday afternoon with the remote and a box of cookies, or a grin and a noogie from the cutest kid you know. It can be as clear and honest as a hand signal you flash when you run into a friend on the street.

On the other hand, peace can be an end to weeks of air attacks by enemy planes. Peace can be liberation from a government that denies you your basic rights. It can be falling asleep on a full stomach for the first time in weeks or seeing your new baby sister make it through her first year without dying.

Sometimes peace is just a moment, a moment you search for every day, a moment of silence and clarity, a moment to close your eyes and listen to the air, a moment free from worrying about what's going to happen next.

Some of us think we experience it all the time; some of us feel like we never quite reach it. But all of us need it.

Peace is something that belongs to us, to each of us. Celebrities, leaders, adults, children, you and me . . . we all have a relationship with peace. And not only that, we all have a responsibility to keep that relationship alive.

Peace is individual, beautiful, and real. But always frustratingly elusive.

What does peace mean to you?

PEACE THEME SONGS

Many people turn to music for peace. The thing is, though, everyone finds peace in different types of music. Hip-hop. Reggae. Techno. Rock and roll. But at the end of the day, if we're all dancing, we're in pretty good shape. Throughout this book you'll find peace anthems nominated by you.

PEACE THEME SONG
"One Love"
performed by
Bob Marley
and The Wailers
Let's get together
And feel alright.
Nominated by
Laura, 18, New York, NY

Check 'em out, hum, bust into an air guitar solo, or whatever. Better yet, come up with your own nomination!

WHaT peace is . . .

ASK DIFFERENT PEOPLE what peace means to them, and you'll get different answers. I know, because I asked you. Here's what you had to say:

Peace is something that can only be achieved through the gift of listening, learning, having an open mind, determination, compassion, and goals of understanding.
—Shaina, 16
Hallowell, Maine

When there is peace we can create.
The greatest civilizations were developed in the seasons when they were in peace.
—Panayiota, 16
Nicosia, Cyprus

It's more than just the absence of war. It is equality and justice. It can be applied to the world, or to one's own personal peace of mind.
—Billy, 18
Rochester, New York

Peace is what happens when the fighting is over, when everyone gets it out of their system and realizes there's only one way to get along, to shut up and listen.
—Mark, 19
New Orleans, Louisiana

Peacefulness, peacefulness, peace-ful-ness
is in the mind of the beholder
—"Peace," performed by **The Roots**

The truly peaceful world would be the one where nobody disliked anybody. You don't have to be all chummy and friendly with someone, but as long as you're not fighting, you're at peace.
—Sarah, 15
Westchester, New York

Peace is safety. If you feel safe, you are at peace.
—Rebecca, 17
Santa Monica, California

When I imagine peace I imagine my family, together. Even if we fight with each other sometimes, we're still together and we love each other and that's what matters.
—Jay, 17
Dallas, Texas

Peace is music. Music is peace.
—Ally, 16
Berkeley, California

Whatever it is, peace is in God's hands.
—Walter, 17
Sasolburg, South Africa

WHaT Peace IS NOT . . .

To UNDERSTAND WHAT PEACE IS, it's sometimes good to think about what it is not. What do you think is the opposite of peace?

"Nonpeace" contains hatred, discrimination, murder of the innocent and non-innocent, stereotypes, racism, sexism, violence, terror. . . . The worst of all is losing hope for peace.
—Omar, 17
Amman, Jordan

Fear.
—Wendy, 19
Durham, North Carolina

Discord and pain.
—Inisia, 17
Mount Vernon, New York

The opposite of peace would be having no power. If you can't do what you want, you're not at peace. Just look at what was going on in Afghanistan. They had no rights and they were in misery.
—Kel, 16
San Diego, California

Having a closed mind. It's weird that people think being closed off brings you peace . . . when all it brings you is anger.
—Alison, 16
Tempe, Arizona

Apathy, a world where no one cares.
—Mat, 17
Rochester, New York

The opposite of peace is confusion. Confusion is dangerous.
—Amanda, 19
Fort Meyers, Florida

It seems to me that violent people are always really angry.
I think the opposite of peace is anger.
—David, 17
Littleton, Colorado

There's a peace inside us all
Let it be your friend
"Inside Us All," performed by **Creed**

Kapayapaan
—TAGALOG

peace places, peace people

WE ALL NEED A BREAK from time to time, to find a quiet moment away from whatever it is that's making us feel stressed out. Some of us retreat into our headphones and lose ourselves in music. Some go for a swim. Some jump in the car and cruise down the highway. Where do you go? Who do you seek out?

> I search for those who bring me ideas. I seek out people who convince me that understanding is possible, that deep down, we share a common pulse.
> —Rachel, 16
> Mercer, Maine

> **When I need peace, I look for myself. Being alone is peaceful.**
> **—David, 17**
> **São Paolo, Brazil**

> When you need peace, you go to your heart . . .
> and try to find out why it is not there.
> —Bojan, 16
> Ohrid, Macedonia

> **Church. Even if there's not a service going on, I know I can go there and sit, silent, and let my thoughts be heard by God.**
> **—Danielle, 15**
> **Denver, Colorado**

When I need peace, I check out my photo albums. All my happy times are in there, and they remind me that things aren't always so crazy in the world.
—Gina, 17
Providence, Rhode Island.

I go to my room. If it's night, I turn off the lights. There is a wonderful view of Istanbul from my window, so I watch Istanbul.
—Burcu, 15
Istanbul, Turkey

I find peace snowboarding and skateboarding.
—Rebecca, 14
San Diego, California

Lying in my boyfriend's arms, candles lighting the room, and listening to music, thinking of nothing at all.
—Rachel, 17
Austin, Texas

When I need peace, I seek out my close friends, who always keep it real with me. They're the only ones who really understand me.
—Cathy, 16
Lansdale, Pennsylvania

I find the ideal place to be is the beach, but it's not always easy to go there.
—Jessye, 17
Brisbane, Australia

When I need some peace and quiet, I go for a run.
Something about losing myself in the challenge of making it through
my five-mile loop makes me forget everything else that's
going on in the world, in my life.
—Adrian, 15
Salt Lake City, Utah

**God. Praying for peace is the best way
to bring it into your life.
—Karen, 19
Antwerp, Belgium**

The "enemy." Talking to your enemy can bring you peace.
—Omar, 17
Amman, Jordan

**When I need peace, I find my mom.
—Sasha, 14
Detroit, Michigan**

—Hindi

*No man's made to stand alone . . .
I just want a happy home*
—"Happy Home," written by **Tupac Shakur**

"This might seem ridiculous, but the person I would like to talk to the most when I need peace is my milkman. You see, in India, 70 percent of the people are completely oblivious to who Usama Bin Laden is; they have not the faintest idea that a building like the World Trade Center ever existed. They are too busy just trying to find enough food to survive. What makes my milkman smile is the fact that his mother had enough food to eat last night. He still dances with joy every time it rains.

It is this simplicity, this innocence of the matters that weigh so heavily on our shoulders, that I wish I could partake in every time my belief in peace is shaken."

—NERGISH, 15
BOMBAY, INDIA

Part Two

Peace
Then

If we don't change our direction,

We're likely to end up where we are going.

—Chinese proverb

—Chinese

The Quest for Peace

TAKE A LOOK at the history of our species and you'll see it: half the time we're trying to keep the peace, the other half of the time we're stirring up trouble.

This is nothing new—you can find wars and massacres in any history book or religious text on the planet. The human race has always lived a paradox: striving for peace on one hand, creating civilizations of violence on the other. This is the challenge we always face when we confront our history and our present.

And we've got to remember that part of striving for peace means acknowledging the wrongs that people, not so different from ourselves, have perpetrated around the world. It's not easy to face these evils, but the knowledge is essential in the pursuit of peace.

February 12, 1996. At a rally in London organized by "Women Involved," people wave paper doves of peace to protest a recent IRA bombing.

There's never been a bloodier century than the one that just ended, the twentieth century. Many more millions were killed or injured in wars, genocides, ethnic cleansings, and political oppression during the twentieth century than at any time before.

Why was it such a violent century? For one thing, the weapons, from tanks to atomic bombs, were more destructive than ever. Also, the population soared, especially in poorer nations, and more people than ever were dissatisfied with their lives, making them more likely to support violent changes. The century was also an era of intense nationalism, when nations often believed that they were better than other nations and were willing to fight to prove it.

And to mix everything up, people migrated, emigrated, and immigrated all over the planet in bigger numbers than ever before. Different groups with different goals found themselves having to deal with one another in new ways—and while for the most part this enriched and enlivened the world, it has also created more conflicts.

For most of the world, the last hundred years were tough. Worldwide, billions of people faced major hardships—including famines, droughts, wars, and other disasters. Hundreds of millions were forced from their homes. Hundreds of millions were denied rights, opportunities, even food. But while wealth continued to grow in some parts of the world, other parts of the world faced greater levels of destitution.

Still, even amid the danger, the hope for peace is alive around the world. We all still have heroes to follow; we still have opportunities to increase the peace. We all can understand and appreciate each other in new ways if we choose to. We're all together on this planet; we're all connected. We just have to learn to work together.

PEACE THEME SONG
"Blowin' in the Wind,"
written by Bob Dylan
How many years can some people exist Before they're allowed to be free?
—nominated by Sarah, 15, Westchester, NY

Mohandas Gandhi ◆ India

"We must be the change we wish to see in this world."

—GANDHI

MOHANDAS GANDHI, often called Mahatma, or "Great Soul," is among the most revered leaders in the history of peace. A leader in India's struggle for independence from Great Britain, Gandhi also worked for peace between rival religious groups (many times, he fasted to promote Hindu and Muslim unity), for racial equality in South Africa,

> *"Generations to come will scarce believe that such a one as this walked the earth in flesh and blood."*
> —ALBERT EINSTEIN, ON MOHANDAS GANDHI

and for an end to the Indian caste system that continues today to keep tens of millions of Indians in hopeless, lifelong poverty.

He was dedicated to nonviolence, inspiring massive marches, sit-ins, boycotts, and strikes (often at great personal risk, as the British considered him a threat to security) for decades before forcing the lowering of the British flag in India in 1947. The modern nation of India, founded on his principles and born on the day the British flag was taken down, remains the world's largest democracy.

Gandhi had a vision for India, and for the entire world, of equality, freedom, and tolerance, all under the umbrella of peace. He absolutely rejected violence in all cases (there is a legend that he wouldn't even harm an insect) and in the process proved that a peaceful movement can overwhelm even the most well-armed and dangerous enemy. He showed that the way to ensure peace is to behave peacefully.

Gandhi was killed in 1948 by a Hindu extremist who felt threatened by Gandhi's policy of peace with Muslims, a man who didn't understand the value of Gandhi's vision.

Gandhi was an inspiration for many future peace leaders around the world, including Martin Luther King, Jr., who traveled to India to meet with Gandhi's followers. Peace leaders today continue to invoke his name with awe and admiration.

✳   ✳   ✳

Gandhi on percussion, Martin Luther King on bass, guitar would be Isaac Newton, keyboards Beethoven, vocals Jesus Christ.

—The Edge, November 10, 2001, when asked to assemble, in his mind, the greatest rock-and-roll band of all time.

"When I speak of love, I am not speaking of some sentimental and weak response. I am speaking of that force which all of the great religions have seen as the supreme unifying principle of life. Love is somehow the key that unlocks the door which leads to ultimate reality."

—MARTIN LUTHER KING, JR.

THERE'S MORE TO THE THIRD MONDAY of January than a day off from school. Martin Luther King Day celebrates a life that changed America, for all of us, for the better.

"Injustice anywhere is a threat to justice everywhere."
—MARTIN LUTHER KING, JR.

In the face of government-imposed segregation, public prejudice, and even the well-armed National Guard, King emulated his hero, Mohandas Gandhi, by leading massive nonviolent sit-ins, boycotts, and strikes in hopes of securing guaranteed civil rights for African Americans. (Granted full citizenship by an amendment to the Constitution in 1863, African Americans were entitled to all the rights and privileges of other Americans, including the right to vote, but in the 1960s much of the southern United States was still heavily segregated. Black Americans were forced to accept lower-paying jobs, given fewer opportunities for education, and forced to use less-sanitary public rest rooms and water fountains. In many towns and counties, their voting rights were denied.)

In the 1950s and 1960s, King traveled tirelessly around the country, leading demonstrations to encourage peace and calm in the struggle for civil rights, including the landmark 1963 March on Washington, where several hundred thousand people heard him deliver his famous "I Have a Dream" speech. Thanks in large part to his hard work the Civil Rights Act, which guaranteed voting rights for blacks across the country, was passed by Congress in 1964.

King knew that the passage of the act was only a first step. Certainly the United States, and the world at large, has yet to achieve complete racial equality, but King led us all closer to that goal than we'd ever been. He understood that he wasn't fighting just for people of his own race. He was fighting for all of us.

Martin Luther King, Jr., was killed by James Earl Ray in 1968 in Memphis, Tennessee.

I'm watching Martin Luther King who had a dream
So take this dream and apply it to your life.
— "New Day," performed by **Wyclef Jean**

Steven Biko ◆ South Africa

"We regard our living together not as an unfortunate mishap warranting endless competition among us, but as a deliberate act of God to make us a community of brothers and sisters."

—STEVEN BIKO

THERE IS ALWAYS MORE THAN ONE FACE OF A MOVEMENT. In the fight against apartheid in South Africa, the great names of Nelson Mandela and Desmond Tutu are the ones most usually associated with the victory. But no less important were the efforts and leadership of Steven Biko.

After growing up under the apartheid system in Eastern Cape, South Africa, Biko founded the Black Consciousness Movement there in 1969 to advocate voting rights and other basic liberties (most of which had been denied to the black South African majority). The movement, which many in the white political system blamed for various acts of terrorism, remained under close scrutiny by the government, and by the mid-1970s Biko had been identified as a threat by an anxious South African government. They began periodically arresting and detaining him, often with little evidence. In 1977 they arrested him for the last time.

Biko died in police custody that year. The government blamed his death on a hunger strike, but after it was revealed that he had sustained major head wounds, they changed their story and blamed Biko's death on a fall during a scuffle. It is now widely believed he was beaten to death by police.

He was 30 years old.

Biko's philosophy says that people must fight internal feelings of inferiority as well as oppression from others. His vision was not the removal of white people from South Africa, but a peaceful, cooperative coexistence where everyone had equal rights and equal opportunities—just like Martin Luther King, Jr., he wanted everyone, not just members of his own race, to live in a peaceful world.

> *You can blow out a candle*
> *But you can't blow out a fire*
> —"Biko," written by **Peter Gabriel**

"My dear young people: I see the light in your eyes, the energy of your bodies and the hope that is your spirit. I know it is you, not I, who will make the future. It is you, not I, who will fix our wrongs and carry forward all that is right with the world."
—NELSON MANDELA, 2001

NELSON MANDELA is perhaps the most famous figure in South African history, a worldwide icon of peace and equality, endurance and commitment.

Born in 1918 in rural South Africa, he had little hope of ever getting a thorough education, let alone of running a country—especially one in which the government was set up specifically to keep him and his race from ever holding any power or even having basic rights, like the right to vote. But young Nelson had parents who pushed him, and he excelled as a student, eventually earning a law degree from the University of South Africa in 1942.

"If out of the tragic events of September 11, the world can find a renewed will to cooperate in finding just solutions to the problems that threaten the safety, security and well-being of us all, the highest tribute would have been paid to those who lost their lives."
—NELSON MANDELA, OCTOBER 2001

After law school, he joined the African National Congress, a new coalition of groups advocating democracy in South Africa. Within a few years the apartheid-sponsoring government considered the ANC, and Mandela specifically, a threat.

They may have had good reason to fear Mandela. After spending the 1950s advocating nonviolent resistance against apartheid, in 1960 Mandela was reported to have organized a more violent arm of the ANC, which was accused of carrying out various terrorist attacks against the government. Mandela went to trial in 1962 and was acquitted of treason charges but was convicted two years later of sabotage and sentenced to life in prison. Many in his country and around the world believed then, and even more believe now, that he was innocent and that he was being held prisoner because of his beliefs, not because of any crimes.

Nelson Mandela spent over 26 years in a South African jail. He was held on an island in a cell with a small window through which he could see, across a channel, to bustling Cape Town, a constant reminder of the world he was being denied. During this time he continued to be the most important worldwide symbol of the struggle against apartheid.

Mandela was released from prison in 1990 and worked closely with the government on the difficult and delicate task of bringing the nation out of apartheid. Mandela was elected president of the Republic of South Africa in 1994. He was awarded the Nobel Peace Prize in 1993.

Hands and feet are all alike
But fear between divides us
— "Cry Freedom," written by **Dave Matthews Band**

Dave Matthews, a native South African who now lives mainly in the United States, has long been a voice for equality and freedom worldwide.

The Nobel Peace Prize

EACH YEAR THE NOBEL COMMITTEE, a Swedish foundation created by scientist Alfred Nobel in 1901, gives out awards in physics, chemistry, medicine, literature, and peace. The Peace Prize is the most famous of the prizes, the most widely respected, and also the most unique.

While the other prizes have very specific goals, to reward scientists or writers for particular contributions to their fields, the Peace Prize is much more subjective. It is awarded each year to the person or group who, according to Nobel's will, "shall have done the most or the best work for fraternity between nations, for the abolition or reduction of standing armies and for the holding and promotion of peace congresses."

Sometimes the prize is awarded for something very specific, like a particular peace agreement, and sometimes it's awarded for years of sustained work.

There have been many famous, and many not so famous, Peace Prize winners over the last 101-plus years. Here are the winners from the past 25.

December 10, 2001. Kofi Annan accepting the Nobel Peace Prize.

2001—Kofi Annan and the United Nations (International)

Annan has been secretary-general of the United Nations since 1997 and has proved to be an incredibly popular leader. He's been especially focused on the problems of young people and on the threat of HIV. He was awarded the prize for his entire range of peaceful work, including helping refugee populations around the world.

2000—Kim Dae Jung (South Korea)

Since the 1950s, Korea has been divided—North Korea is a totalitarian state, much like Cuba (only poorer); South Korea is more democratic. Kim, president of South Korea, is known for his attempts to reconcile with the north, summed up in his "Sunshine Policy," which, among other things, allows South Korean families to attempt to reunite with relatives across the border.

The back of the Nobel Peace Medal. The inscription reads, "For peace and brotherhood of men."

1999—Doctors Without Borders (International)

Doctors Without Borders is an international group of volunteer doctors who bring medical care to people who would otherwise probably never see it. In the 1990s they served in Rwanda, Zaire, Bosnia, Chechnya, and other places at war.

1998—John Hume and David Trimble (Northern Ireland)

Hume and Trimble, political leaders from opposite sides of the ongoing Protestant-versus-Catholic struggle in their homeland, brought about a cease-fire in Northern Ireland called the Good Friday Agreement. The agreement eventually led to a promise by Catholic guerrilla soldiers to disarm themselves completely.

1997—Jody Williams and the International Campaign to Ban Land Mines (International)

Williams and her group were awarded the prize for their continuing work to educate world leaders about the dangers of land mines and to encourage nations to cease production of these deadly weapons, which kill more children than soldiers. (See page 122.)

1996—Carlos Felipe Ximenes Belo and Jose Ramos-Horta (East Timor)

Belo, the cardinal of predominantly Catholic East Timor, a small Asian nation, and Ramos-Horta, permanent representative to the United Nations for East Timor helped secure independence for East

Timor, which had been occupied and oppressed by mostly Islamic Indonesia since 1975.

1995—Joseph Rotblat (Great Britain), Pugwash Conferences on Science and World Affairs (Canada)

Rotblat, a Polish physicist who escaped Nazi occupation and relocated to Great Britain, and the Pugwash conferences he helped create in Canada, were awarded the prize for bringing together scientists and world leaders to work toward reducing the threat of nuclear war worldwide.

1994—Yasser Arafat (Palestine) and Shimon Peres (Israel)

Arafat and Peres won after signing a peace agreement that helped secure Israel's sovereignty while also giving more freedoms to Palestinians living under Israeli rule. The peace was relatively short-lived, and the area is still in upheaval, with many killed in the first few months of 2002 alone.

1993—Nelson Mandela and Frederik Willem de Klerk (South Africa)

Mandela (see page 28), an anti-apartheid leader, and de Klerk, president of South Africa, were awarded the prize for their combined efforts to end apartheid in South Africa.

1992—Rigoberta Menchú Tum (Guatemala)

Menchú Tum, a descendant of the Mayan people (an important native Central American civilization that was overrun and enslaved by the Spanish in the sixteenth century) organized her people to resist the Spanish-speaking government's mistreatment and shed light on the struggle of indigenous people in Central and South America. (See page 120.)

1991—Daw Aung San Suu Kyi (Myanmar)

Daw Aung San Suu Kyi won for her nonviolent resistance to the military regime in her homeland. (See page 116.)

1990—Mikhail Gorbachev (Russia)

Gorbachev won for returning independence to lands conquered and annexed by the Soviet Union, an oppressive communist superpower. Fifteen nations regained their independence as a result of his leadership, including Kazakhstan, Georgia, Armenia, Ukraine, and Lithuania.

1989—Tenzin Gyatso, the Fourteenth Dalai Lama (Tibet)

The Dalai Lama, spiritual leader of Tibet, has dedicated his life to educating the world about the oppressive political situation in his homeland. (See page 118.)

May 31, 1988. Soviet leader Mikhail Gorbachev and U.S. President Ronald Reagan take an impromptu walk through Red Square in Moscow, then part of the Soviet Union.

1988—United Nations Peacekeeping Forces (International)

The UN peacekeeping forces won for their efforts at keeping the peace in politically unstable places, including the Middle East, parts of Africa, Southeast Asia, and the Balkans.

1987—Oscar Arias Sanchez (Costa Rica)

Sanchez, president of Costa Rica, won for creating a peace plan that ended the civil war in the neighboring country of Guatemala. The prize also recognized his leadership of his homeland of Costa Rica, known for being the most stable nation in Central America. Costa Rica also has no standing army.

1986—Elie Weisel (United States)

Weisel spent his life writing about his experiences in concentration camps during World War II and working for the rights and empowerment of Jews and other oppressed groups.

1985—International Physicians for the Prevention of Nuclear War, Inc. (International)

This global group of doctors was awarded the prize for educating world leaders and the public about the horrors the world would face if there were a nuclear war.

1984—Desmond Tutu (South Africa)

Tutu, a Catholic bishop and one of the most prominent black South African leaders, worked tirelessly to end the oppressive apartheid system in South Africa without using violence.

1983—Lech Walesa (Poland)

A popular leader of factory workers, Walesa helped inspire the Polish people to get out from under the political control of the Soviet Union, which occupied Poland after World War II.

1982—Alva Myrdal (Sweden) and Alfonso García Robles (Mexico)

These two scholar-diplomats were given the award to honor the dozens of years of dedication shown in the pursuit of peace. They both worked for decades with the UN and governments around the world, educating leaders about the dangers of weapons buildup worldwide.

1981—Office of the United Nations High Commissioner for Refugees (International)

This group (which also won the prize in 1954) focuses all its efforts on helping refugees around the world. In 1982 the biggest refugee crises in the world were Ethiopia, Vietnam, and Afghanistan. (Sound familiar?)

1980—Adolfo Pérez Esquivel (Argentina)

Esquivel, a political activist (as well as a successful sculptor and architect) worked to bring an end to the terrorism and military law that had kept Argentina in a state of panic throughout much of the 1970s.

1979—Mother Teresa (India)

Mother Teresa, a Macedonian nun who joined the Sisters of Loreto in Calcutta, India, devoted her life to satisfying the basic human needs of and bringing basic human rights to the poorest people in India, traditionally called "untouchables." Her example still inspires people, especially the Sisters of Loreto, to continue the fight against poverty.

1978—Muhammad Anwar al-Sadat (Egypt) and Menachem Begin (Israel)

Sadat, president of Egypt, was the first leader of an Arabic nation to conduct talks with Israel, a traditional enemy of the predominantly Islamic states in the region. Begin, prime minister of Israel, welcomed and encouraged the opportunity to ease tensions. Begin and Sadat worked for and signed a peace agreement, and the two nations haven't fought since.

1977—Amnesty International (International)

Amnesty International is a group of volunteers who work to bring public attention and legal help to people being held in jail for political reasons instead of criminal ones. They're still a powerful force worldwide.

"No one is born a good citizen; no nation is born a democracy. Rather, both are processes that continue to evolve over a lifetime. Young people must be included from birth. A society that cuts itself off from its youth severs its lifeline."
—KOFI ANNAN, UN SECRETARY-GENERAL
AND RECIPIENT OF THE 2001 NOBEL PEACE PRIZE

Peace in the Twentieth Century

OF COURSE, THE HISTORY OF PEACE is a complicated one . . . nothing is ever quite as easy as it seems, and what is peace to one side of a conflict may not feel like peace to another side. But there have been some especially remarkable moments throughout the past 100 years or so. Here are just a few.

1901 | The Nobel Peace Prize is established in Sweden. The first year saw two winners: Jean Henri Dumont (Switzerland), who founded the International Committee of the Red Cross in the nineteenth century, and Frederic Passey (France), who worked with European governments to end the war between France and Prussia. (For more on the Peace Prize, see page 30.)

1919 | As World War I ends, the Paris Peace Conference opens. Leaders of Britain, Italy, France, and the United States begin the process of stabilizing Europe. Ultimately The Paris conference will lead to the 1924 founding of the League of Nations—a predecessor to the current United Nations. American president Woodrow Wilson is the leading visionary behind the founding of the league.

1945 | World War II, which pitted the United States and its allies against Germany, Italy, and Japan, ends after six years of fighting and millions of deaths and injuries. Europe is divided into the mostly democratic West and the mostly communist East, which is held under tight control by the Soviet Union. Japan is demilitarized. To

1949. First Lady Eleanor Roosevelt, U.S., holding a poster of The Universal Declaration of Human Rights.

promote a climate of peace in the world, the United States, the Soviet Union, Great Britain, France, China, and dozens of other nations meet in San Francisco to form the United Nations. A more modern, more global version of the League of Nations, the UN quickly becomes, and remains, the most respected diplomatic organization on the planet.

| 1947 | The Indian subcontinent, under the nonviolent leadership of Mohandas Gandhi (see page 22), secures total independence from Great Britain and is partitioned into India and Pakistan. Jawaharlal Nehru becomes the first prime minister of multicultural India, now the world's largest democracy, and voting rights are extended to all citizens. Pakistan becomes the world's second-largest Islamic republic. Leaders continue to work to ease tensions between the rival nations. |

| 1948 | Israel declares independence as a Jewish state. While Israel survives the century under constant threat from its predominantly Muslim neighbors, several steps toward coexistence and peace are accomplished, including the 1978 Camp David accords, which ends fighting between Israel and Egypt, and the 1994 Camp David agreement, which grants more independence, land, and self-rule to Palestinians in Israeli-controlled territories. |

| 1957 | Ghana, a British colony, becomes the first African nation to gain independence from European rule. In the 30 years that follow, over 40 African nations declare independence from colonial rulers like Great Britain, Portugal, Italy, France, Belgium, and Germany. Many nations have struggled since declaring their independence, but many, including South Africa, Gambia, Zimbabwe, and Kenya, have especially hopeful futures. |

1961   President Kennedy founds the Peace Corps, sending young Americans around the world to help bring education and skills to impoverished nations. Besides helping to build shelter and improve food and water supplies in dozens of countries around the globe, the corps helps bring young Americans face-to-face with people from other cultures and backgrounds.

March 1, 1961. President Kennedy signs the document that would create the Peace Corps.

1964   The Civil Rights Act is signed in Congress. The law requires local governments across the United States to guarantee and enforce the right to vote for all citizens. While blacks had been awarded the right to vote over 100 years earlier, in many parts of the country, especially in the South, local governments made it remarkably difficult for blacks to exercise that right. Martin Luther King, Jr. (see page 24) was the primary force behind a nationwide movement to pass this law. Until his assassination in 1968, King continued to focus on peace and equality for all, in schools, in government, in jobs, and everywhere.

1965–75   Massive antiwar demonstrations rock the United States, which becomes increasingly involved in the Vietnam War. Over 600,000 American soldiers are in the area by 1968, the same year a half-million peace demonstrators march on Washington, D.C. Thousands of Americans, and millions of Southeast Asians, die in the decades-long guerrilla fighting between communist-supported North Vietnam and western-supported democratic South Vietnam. In 1975, the United States withdraws from the region. Over the next decade millions are killed and displaced in Vietnam, Cambodia, and Laos as militaristic governments take over. Citizens from around the world rally for peace in Southeast Asia almost daily during this period.

1969 The United States and the Soviet Union, embroiled in an arms race since World War II, begin nuclear-arms-reduction discussions, which result in the SALT (Strategic Arms Limitation Talks) agreement of 1972, limiting production of certain types of nuclear missiles.

1971 George Harrison of the Beatles organizes the Concert for Bangladesh, held in New York City as a benefit. The nation, formerly under Pakistani control, had just gained independence after over 3 million of its people were killed by the Pakistani military but was facing severe famine. The concert, which raised funds for the country and also raised awareness around the world about what was going on there, features Harrison, Ringo Starr, Eric Clapton, Ravi Shankar, and others.

1972 Richard Nixon becomes the first U.S. president to visit China, a communist, totalitarian regime. He holds historic meetings with Chinese leader Mao Tse-Tung. The visit finally breaks the 24-year-old official silence between the two nations and begins a dialogue that continues today.

1978   The American Indian Movement (AIM) stages a march from Alcatraz Island in San Francisco Bay to Washington, D.C., to encourage the U.S. government to grant more land rights to Native Americans.

Russel Means, a Lakota Sioux Indian and principal leader of the American Indian Movement, holds his son, Tatanka.

1979   Dozens of rallies, marches, sit-ins, and other events are held around the United States in the most active anti-nuclear protest year on record. In one of the largest gatherings, over 200,000 people rally in New York City. The SALT II agreement between the United States and the Soviet Union, which further restricts nuclear arms, is signed.

1985   Live Aid, the biggest-ever fund-raising concert, raises millions for famine and drought victims in Ethiopia, Sudan, and other African regions. Held in London and Philadelphia and televised around the world, the 24-hour concert features performances by Black Sabbath, Run DMC, Sting, U2, The Who, Elton John, Madonna, Duran Duran, and Bob Dylan. It's considered the model for all subsequent televised fund-raisers, including the various efforts after September 11, 2001.

1989 The Berlin Wall, which for 30 years had divided communist East Berlin from democratic West Berlin, comes down. Germany is unified under one government for the first time in almost 50 years.

Nov. 10, 1989. Berliners sing and dance on top of the Berlin Wall to celebrate the opening of East-West German borders. Thousands of East German citizens moved into the West after East German authorities opened all border crossing points to the West. In the background is the Brandenburg Gate.

1989 Apartheid is abolished in South Africa, guaranteeing voting and civil rights for blacks as well as whites. Although the transition is sometimes difficult, the world throws its support behind the new multicultural coalition government.

1989 Hundreds of thousands of Chinese citizens rally in the streets of Beijing for increased civil and economic freedoms. (See page 106.) Chinese leaders crack down on the protesters, but the number of people supporting the cause continues to grow.

1990	Soviet leader Mikhail Gorbachev begins the breakup of the communist superpower known as the Soviet Union. Over 15 new nations are established in Europe and Central Asia as Russia relaxes control. Gorbachev is awarded the Nobel Peace Prize.
1991	Following the Iraqi invasion of Kuwait, the United States leads an international force in driving the Iraqi army out and restoring the status quo to the region. The United States becomes more deeply involved in the struggle to maintain peace in the area.
1996	Seventy-one members of the United Nations, including the United States, China, France, Russia, and Great Britain, sign the Nuclear Test Ban Treaty, agreeing to refrain from testing nuclear weapons.

April 1, 1996. A group of anti-nuke activists demonstrate outside the U.S. Department of Energy offices in Las Vegas.

1997 Pol Pot, despotic ruler of Cambodia during the 1970s and widely considered the mastermind behind over 2 million deaths (20 percent of his nation's population), is captured in a Southeast Asian jungle. He dies before he can stand trial.

Cambodian boys play on a wall at Angkor Wat temple complex in Siem Reap, Cambodia. During the reign of Pol Pot, this amazing historical site was cut off from most of the world.

1998 The Good Friday agreement in Ireland signals the beginning of a formalized, speedy peace process between both sides in the Irish conflict, the Republicans (mostly Catholic) and the Loyalists (mostly Protestant). (See page 102.)

1999 The Serbian military is ousted from Kosovo by UN forces and American bombing raids. Serbian leaders were responsible for the deaths of hundreds of thousands of Muslims in the Balkan peninsula during the 1990s as they sought to promote their own race and culture. United Nations peacekeeping forces are brought into the region to help ease tensions, and President Milosevic of Serbia is put on trial for war crimes.

peace past

IF YOU LOOK JUST AT NUMBERS, they tell us that around the world, more people are involved in more wars now than ever before in history. But for many of us numbers don't really mean much . . . what means something are people's individual experiences. We all have a different relationship with the world, and we all see it in a different light, based on our own lives and experiences.

People in the United States feel differently than others around the world, people in older generations feel differently than teenagers, people at some high schools feel differently than others. Do you believe we're living in a more peaceful world today?

My grandfather was in the army, and he went to Korea. He's always talking about how tough it was. He's lived through some wars—World War II, Korea, and Vietnam—where so many people he knew, or knew about, died. I've only lived through the Gulf War and now the War on Terrorism, but I don't know anyone who even went to those wars. I think our lives are definitely more peaceful today.
—Aaron, 15
Goleta, California

There is so much hatred today, and so many weapons to show how big the hatred is. That makes the world a lot less peaceful.
—Bojan, 16
Ohrid, Macedonia

—ITALIAN, ROMANIAN

I always assumed it was more peaceful. But now I realize that's because I'm lucky enough not to live in a war zone.
—Elliott, 17
Denver, Colorado

It's more peaceful in some aspects and in some it's worse. With modern technology it's easier for people to communicate and easier to terrorize people.
—Sasha, 14
Ann Arbor, Michigan

People still hate each other just as much as they always did. They just disguise it better now.
—Mia, 17
Uppsala, Sweden

No matter what, it's not peaceful enough. We need to make better choices.
—David, 17
São Paolo, Brazil

PEACE THEME SONG
"One,"
performed by Creed
We may rise and fall,
but in the end
We meet our fate together
—nominated by Shaina, 16,
Hallowell, Maine

Part Three

Peace
Now

My mind goes to young people at a time
like this. That's really the only way to say it.

—Bob Dylan

—Hebrew

New World

NO DOUBT ABOUT IT, it's a new world now. Although many of us were able to ignore it before the September 11, 2001, attacks, the world was swiftly becoming more complex, and more dangerous, than ever.

But on that day everything changed. Suddenly we woke up.

The attacks saw thousands of Americans, and people from around the world, die. Over 3,000 in New York City. Almost 200 in Washington, D.C. Dozens in Pennsylvania.

But we also saw hundreds of millions of Americans, and billions of people around the world, come together with a single purpose in a way like never before. For a moment it didn't matter who we were or where we came from—we were all in it together. Strangers became family.

And suddenly our heroes weren't pop stars who sang about puppy love; they were firefighters who gave their lives to rescue people they'd never seen before. They were rescue workers struggling to free survivors and to search for those less lucky. They were friends and family members left behind, holding on to hope as long as they could.

But almost as soon as we united behind these heroes, the world began to wonder. What did we all come together for? To fight terrorism? To punish the perpetrators? To flex our muscles?

Or did we come together to build a new world, a smarter world?

Yes, we live in a frightening time. But it's a time of unbelievable opportunity. When the world collapses, we get to decide who our heroes are. And as long as we have heroes, we have hope.

PEACE THEME SONG
"Only Time,"
performed by Enya
Who can say
Where the road goes?
—nominated by
Roni, 17, Haifa, Israel

March 16, 2002. New York City firefighters observe a moment of silence for the victims of the World Trade Center Attacks during the St. Patrick's Day Parade.

No time for indecision
We got to make a move

—"Let's Roll"
written by Neil Young

March 11, 2002. People pay respects at the temporary crash site memorial for victims of United Flight 93, which crashed September 11, 2001 outside Shanksville, Pa.

NEIL YOUNG WROTE "LET'S ROLL" as a tribute to Todd Beamer and the other heroes of United Airlines Flight 93. For almost fifteen minutes Beamer stayed on an in-flight phone with a 911 operator, giving a full account of everything he saw and heard on the flight. Hijackers had taken control of the plane (it is now believed they intended to crash it into the White House or Camp David), so Beamer and the others, who knew about the earlier attacks by plane at the World Trade Center, decided to rush the hijackers and force a crash landing in the Pennsylvania country-side. All 45 on board were killed, but it's impossible to know how many were saved by preventing the plane from reaching its intended target.

"Let's roll" was Todd's catchphrase and it was the last thing he was heard saying into the phone.

WHere were you?

WE ALL HAVE A STORY about September 11, 2001. We all remember where we were, who we were with, and how we felt. We were horrified, sad, afraid. We were confused. We didn't know what to feel.

Some stories are more dramatic, some bigger, some more outlandish than others. One person's story might be hopeful; another's might be pessimistic. Some may feel distant and removed. But all of our stories are important. By remembering our stories, the big and the small, the famous and the unknown, and by remembering the day it all happened, we can help ensure it'll never happen again.

What's *your* story?

> I was walking home from school when my mother picked me up and told me the news. I couldn't stop crying for about an hour. How could anyone with a heart do this? I remembered standing on top of those towers when I was younger, looking down on New York, and I kept imagining the fear I would have felt looking down and seeing a plane below me flying into the building. I hope I will never feel that kind of fear, but now I cannot be sure.
> —Charlotte, 16
> London, United Kingdom

> I never understood why teenagers beat each other at school, insult each other, all of that. I could never understand why we all acted this way. But that changed. I saw many people at school who were enemies on Monday, September 10, but best friends on Tuesday, September 11.
> —Amanda, 15
> Columbia, South Carolina

I was sitting in class, bored out of my mind. I thought about how my teacher's plaid shirt was the same one my father was wearing that morning. It looked like a place mat. I didn't like it. Five minutes earlier I had been down in the gym, getting my school pictures taken. I was sure they came out awful. All of a sudden another teacher was at the window, waving her arms, and our teacher ran out. They exchanged whispers, and he came back in the room. "The Pentagon has been bombed, they believe, and one of the World Trade Center towers is on fire. They believe there will be more attacks. No one knows exactly what's going on; we'll just have to wait and see."

—Shaina, 16
Hallowell, Maine

It felt like the world was ending that day because it seemed like no one knew what to do. But when I got home from school, I found out that my good friend's mom gave birth to a perfect baby boy. So I guess there's always joy, even when things are horrible.
—Cortney, 16
Spartanburg, South Carolina

For the first part of the day, they didn't even tell us what was going on in school. We knew something was up because there were all these rumors flying around, like we were being nuked, but I figured everyone was just exaggerating, that it was just some plane crash or something. I didn't realize how bad things were until I got home. My friend told me that gas prices were soaring, so I went to the nearest gas station and waited in a half-mile line to fill up the tank. While I was waiting, all I could think about was I wished I could do something to help.

—Christine, 16
Columbus, Ohio

—TELUGU

54

At first it seemed like a normal day. I woke up, shut off my alarm, and went upstairs to grab some breakfast. My dad was walking back and forth and yelling into the phone like he was mad at something. My mom was sitting, being very quiet. I could see the news was on, but I didn't know what they were talking about. I asked Mom, "What's wrong with Daddy?" and she said, "A real tragic thing happened in New York City." I was so confused. I looked at the TV and saw people jumping out of windows and wondered what they were thinking on the way down.
—Micaela, 13
Kernersville, North Carolina

That night was supposed to be my first violin recital. Of course it was canceled. I couldn't pick up my violin the whole rest of the week because I knew I couldn't make it sound right.
—Val, 15
Washington, D.C.

One of my close friends cried all day because her dad is in the navy. I remember students saying that the solution was to nuke or bomb whoever had done this. I remember feeling alone because I was confused and didn't think the answer was to hurt anyone else. Enough people had died.
—Shannon, 17
Zionsville, Indiana

The strangest thing was how other kids in my school were trying to figure out who would be next that day. Chicago? Houston? California? My hometown? I was afraid.
—Alison, 17
Minneapolis, Minnesota

Even though my parents don't work in New York or anything, my initial reaction was to call them and make sure everyone was all right. Hearing my parents' voices was like sugar. My mom came and picked me up from school, and I spent the rest of the day with her.
—Collette, 16
Mountain Lakes, New Jersey

I was at school, in the library, when I heard. I was starting a project on world energy consumption, so my mind was already focused on the Middle East, which is where much of the world's oil comes from. My friend and I heard kids yelling about what was happening, and when we saw the TV, we went numb. To this day, I am still numb about it, and I still don't understand, no matter how much people explain it. I think I would have to visit the actual site in New York to even begin to understand.
—Ashley, 18
Ontario, Canada

What really made me scared was when my teacher couldn't even explain it to us. He just stood there watching the TV with the rest of the class. We kept asking him why, and he didn't know what to say.
—Cat, 15
Columbus, Ohio

PEACE THEME SONG
"Wonderful,"
written by
Everclear
I feel better when
I hear them say
Everything will be
wonderful someday
—nominated by Lela, 15,
Ann Arbor, Michigan

The first person who said anything about the attacks was a substitute teacher. We were passing him in the hallway, and he said something about two planes crashing into the World Trade Center. In my mind I was thinking, "That's really sad, but stuff like this happens every day. It's not like it's anything new." I just didn't get it.

It wasn't until three hours later that I really understood what had happened. I felt so completely horrible. How could I have just shrugged off this terrible tragedy without giving it a second thought? More people died in the towers than the population of my whole entire small town.

Later that day we were still watching the news. Soon kids started complaining about watching it. They said they were bored. I wasn't, though. I couldn't tear my eyes away from the TV screen, showing the suffering of people a thousand miles away.
—Marcie, 14
Dial, Texas

I stayed home from school that day. I was on-line talking to my friends, and they told me about a tragedy, but I didn't think much of it because I am rarely ever moved by anything. But later on, I was watching TV and I saw the footage. For the first time in my life I had a sense of fear. My dad is in the military, and during the Kosovo situation we lived in Germany and I was never scared, but that day, I felt so vulnerable. I was all alone and couldn't get my brother or mother or anyone on the phone. My brother is 18 and my best friend, he's 17 . . . and they are just the type of people to go sign up if they're needed to fight a war. I was really scared for them. But at the same time I wanted to fight for my country, too.
—Natalie, 16
Oklahoma City, Oklahoma

When I heard about the terrorist attacks, I immediately thought about my brother and sister-in-law. They lived less than four blocks away from the World Trade Center. All that I could do was wonder if they were all right. In the middle of sixth period my dad, who works at the school I go to, came to my class and told me that Brady and Jess were fine when the planes hit the towers, but Jess's parents didn't know what happened to them after the towers fell. On the bus home from school, the radio had an estimated death toll, and the angry tears I had been holding back all that day came rushing down my face. Once I got home, I headed straight for the TV. I turned on the news and didn't change the channel for nearly six hours.

Later that night my family was overjoyed when they heard from my brother and sister-in-law. We found out that the only thing that kept my brother out of the subway underneath the towers was the fact that he and his wife overslept. When they were evacuated, they grabbed a change of clothes for each of them, the cell phone, and the dog. After they left the building, they had to board a ferry to New Jersey.

They had trouble getting to Jess's parents' house because everyone at the train station was giving them trouble about the dog. My sister-in-law even had an argument with a police officer there. She had to explain to them that she wasn't just taking their dog for a ride, but that they were evacuated out of their apartment.
—Courtney, 13
Houston, Texas

I was in driver's ed class when they made an announcement, "There has been a terrorist attack on the Twin Towers." My teacher played it off and made it sound like it was no big deal. Then a few minutes later they came on again and said, "We understand many of you have relatives in New York, so if you feel the need to come down to the office and make phone calls, please do." I knew something weird was going on, but I wasn't too scared until I found out they hit the Pentagon, too. My father lives in D.C., so from then on I was petrified . . . for all I knew, they were hitting every big building in D.C. It was the worst feeling of my life, not to know if everyone in my family was safe. Until I heard from my dad, everything was chaos, and I never want to feel that way ever again.

—Chelsea, 15
Cherry Hill, New Jersey

Where were you when the world stopped turning
On that September day?
—"Where Were You (When the World Stopped Turning)?"
written by **Alan Jackson**

september in New York

BEFORE IT BECAME GROUND ZERO, the World Trade Center district in New York was a place that many thousands of people passed through every day. Besides being home to many schools, the area is a major transportation hub, and one of the few malls in Manhattan used to be just below the towers.

They say everyone was affected by the events, and that's true. But people were affected differently, even people who were near the World Trade Center at the time. Check out these reactions from New York City.

> I was sure I was going to die.
> —Caprial, 16
> Manhattan

I lost two friends that were police officers. It is very hard to cope. Any reminder of this tragic event makes me want to break down and cry. My home has been hit, but we are strong.
—Alicia, 18
Manhattan

> Today I cried more than yesterday. But the day before that, I hardly cried at all. I never know when I'm going to cry anymore.
> —Tania, 16
> Manhattan

When one of the psychiatrists came to my class and told us we could talk to him about anything, no one really went to him. No one knew what to say. He just sort of sat there.
—Edward, 16
Manhattan

September 11 had to be one of the scariest and most confusing days of my life. I go to Hunter College in Manhattan. After my morning class I came out to meet my friends, and one of them told me what happened. None of the public phones were working or anyone's cell, so it was impossible to call my family. I live in Queens, about twenty minutes away, but since they closed the bridges and subway and everything, there was no way for me to get home. I went with a friend of mine to church, where we found some comfort and tranquility in what was now a city of chaos. I wish to never live through something like that again.

—Nina, 18
Queens

I leaned on my friends and classmates more that day than I ever had before. Even my teachers felt like friends. It seemed like no one really could explain why it was all happening, but being with my friends and people I knew made it seem like things were going to be all right.
—Carrie, 15
Manhattan

I've never been so scared in my life. But I knew that whatever happened, I would be able to follow it up and define myself.
—Charlotte, 18
Manhattan

PEACE THEME SONG
"Freedom,"
written by
Jimi Hendrix
Freedom, that's what
I need now
Freedom to live
—nominated by Cameron, 19,
Los Angeles, California

Amani
—SWAHILI

I was in my dorm room, just a few blocks from the World Trade Center. I was getting dressed for an interview for an internship when my roommate's mother called and wanted to know where my roommate was. I told her she'd already left, and her mom then told me to turn on the TV, quick. I flipped it on and saw the flames and smoke. I was staring at the TV, still on the phone, when the second plane hit. The apartment shook. I grabbed my stuff and left the apartment, and when I got outside, the street was filling with smoke, ash, and broken glass. I went to the subway, still in shock. When I showed up at the interview, everyone was leaving the office and looking at me like I was crazy. It wasn't until then that I heard the word terrorism. They let me call my family in California. Only then did I begin to cry.
—Jennifer, 21
Manhattan

I remember that my friend Mary Ann had to leave class that morning because she had a friend on the 90-something floor in the World Trade Center that day, and she didn't know if she was all right. I waited at school for my parents, who came to pick me up, and when we went outside, I could smell the smoke and I saw cars covered in ash. Mary Ann still hasn't heard from her friend.
—Deena, 16
Brooklyn

—DUTCH, FLEMISH, AFRIKAANS

I'M NOT AFRAID TO VISIT NEW YORK.
—Sign held up by teen visitor outside *The Today Show*

Stuyvesant High School

THOUSANDS OF TEENS were in New York when the towers came down. Many of them were in class at Stuyvesant High School—just blocks away from the World Trade Center. Stuyvesant High School ("Stuy" to its students) is considered to be among the finest public high schools in New York City.

On September 11 the school was evacuated shortly after the second plane crash, and the student body was instructed to walk north, away from the site of the attacks. While some students scrambled to pay phones to hear news of family members who worked in the towers, others reported to volunteer stations to begin helping out with the relief effort.

Stuyvesant High School, because it is so close to Ground Zero, was designated as a staging area for rescue workers, medical crews, and relief workers. Many people were treated for injuries there.

Its students were sent to another school in Brooklyn, where they could resume classes until their building was no longer needed and until it had been inspected for structural damage and air quality.

Like tens of thousands of people who lived and worked in or near the World Trade complex, these students had to move forward with their lives under intense pressure—not only were they worried about loved ones and fearful about what might happen next, but they had to go through it in unfamiliar surroundings. Just dealing every day was an amazing act of bravery. It was over 10 weeks before students were able to return to their own building.

PEACE THEME SONG

"Let It Be," written by John Lennon and Paul McCartney
There's still a light that shines on me
Shine until tomorrow
—nominated by Burcu, 15, Istanbul, Turkey

After being besieged nonstop by reporters and broadcasters, many of the students at Stuy were weary of reliving September 11, 2001. Students were relieved when the administration decided the school would no longer officially participate in media

Oct. 16, 2001. This "Tree of Life" banner has "tree of life" painted in 30 different languages on it. It was created by the students of Stuyvesant High School and unfurled on the side of their school.

interviews. Like everyone across the country, students at Stuy wanted to get back to work because, as students trying to stick to a normal routine, they still had papers and exams and extracurriculars to take care of. As one student told *The New York Times* in November 2001, "We are over it now. We really don't have time to think about it."

"Over it"? Maybe that sounds a little harsh. Sure, it's hard to believe any of us will ever really be over it. We'll never be the same, and we'll never forget. But in times when the world turns upside down, it's amazing how something normal like a midterm can seem, somehow, comforting.

celebrities Reflect

THE TRAGEDY OF SEPTEMBER 11, 2001, erased, for a moment, distinctions between celebrities and noncelebrities. Money, status, and fame ceased to matter as everyone, no matter how celebrated, struggled to understand what was going on. Here's what some celebrities were thinking after the tragedy.

I felt so trivial and so confused and so extraordinarily lost. I've never had to do my job in a time of war, and I don't know how to do my job right now, and I'm learning literally in front of you, and that is very humiliating and embarrassing because you just do feel trivial at a time like this.

— **DREW BARRYMORE**

I am an immigrant—everybody is, except for the indigenous people, of course. I'm so disappointed when I hear people starting to divide America up into who is American and who isn't.

— **DAVE MATTHEWS**

Getting onstage was hard. But performing was like therapy for us and the audience.

— **KEVIN RICHARDSON**
OF THE BACKSTREET BOYS

I feel like everyone who died in that building was part of me. The thing that keeps goin' through my head is the phoenix that rises out of the ashes. Although there's despair and confusion, that's definitely not the end of the world, and it's not gonna stop us.

— **ALICIA KEYS**

The structure itself means nothing to me. I don't believe in that structure being a symbol of power, of pride, of America. What means something to me is the people that were killed around and in that building innocently, for no reason except hatred. It overwhelms me.

—FRED DURST OF LIMP BIZKIT

Sure, if they needed me to fight terrorists in the military, I'd go.

—LANCE BASS OF *NSYNC

We didn't want people to think we meant it as a sign of disrespect, but we decided to go ahead because maybe we could in a small way help people start the renewal process. We need to continue with what makes us happy and what reminds us that we're alive. Music does that for a lot of people.

—BRANDON BOYD, LEAD SINGER OF INCUBUS, ON HIS BAND'S DECISION TO PERFORM IN NEW YORK JUST DAYS AFTER THE ATTACKS

There's no amount of anger that could justify such a slaughter.

—TRENT REZNOR OF NINE INCH NAILS

I used to see the Twin Towers perfectly, right outside my window. Now I look and it's just emptiness. It looks just like smoke and nothing. That's very different and difficult, but basically, I'm here. I'm a New Yorker, and I'm staying.

—MARIAH CAREY

—FRENCH

In September 2001, we were in London mixing our Rock Steady album, and at that point we were just flying high . . . everything in the world was great! We were almost done and then we came into work one day and it had happened and we were like, whoa. It felt really weird to be out of the country. And the project we were working on felt so insignificant and inappropriate and we were like, well, maybe we shouldn't put this out this year.

After we had a little time and came home and everything, we realized this was the perfect record to put out . . . that people wanted to feel good. The first show that we did was in October, opening for U2 at Madison Square Garden [in New York City], so that was pretty spectacular. We felt like we had something to give all these people who were brave enough to come out. It was like a night of healing.

There was a moment of fear when I was supposed to go to the VH1 fashion awards in November. I was like, I don't have to go to these, they're so not important. But if nobody goes, then nobody does anything and that just means we're all just sitting around. I kinda felt like I should just go for it. Not that it was risking my life, but I just kinda felt like I should.

It's like proving a point, not letting it change your life.

—GWEN STEFANI, LEAD SINGER OF NO DOUBT

FRED

—DANISH, NORWEGIAN, AND SWEDISH

eve speaks out

IN THE COURSE OF TALKING to all of you, and listening to your points of view on-line and in person, I also managed to score a few minutes with Eve, who inspires many of us with her determination, confidence, and strength. Turns out she had a lot to say about peace and its place in this troubled world.

How do you define peace?

For me, it's about inner peace. Everyone has to have that. Once you have that, then you can deal with everything else. You have to be able to deal with yourself first. If you can do that, you can move on.

Inner peace is something that everyone has to find on their own. For me, it's about God. But not everyone believes in religion, so they have to find it themselves. I really believe, though, that the only way to get to a peaceful world is for people to develop their own personal sense of peace. (Laughs) I sound like such a hippie right now, and I'm only 23. But seriously, if everyone was more comfortable in their own skin, the world would be a better place.

Where do you go when you lose your personal sense of peace?

I make sure I have some time alone, every day. In my hotel room, or at home, or whatever. I make sure I'm alone. So I can think, breathe, clear my mind. Sometimes I'll be in silence, sometimes I'll just stare into the TV. But I do it every day.

Do you consider your world a peaceful one?

Definitely. It's hard to keep it that way. I try not to involve entertainment in my personal life. But it's a struggle, because there are just so many people at you as soon as you get up in the morning. But I'm a big kid, so I keep it separate.

Who do you seek out when you need peace?

God. I talk to him at all times. I *know* he's sick of me, 'cause I'm talking to him all the time.

My family wasn't very religious. But I tried a lot of different religions. I went through Jehovah's Witnesses, I tried to be a Baptist, I went to Catholic school and thought I wanted to be Catholic, then I tried Sunni Islam . . . and I really liked it. It was peaceful to me. It was simple. But it would be so hypocritical of me to be onstage and pretend to be practicing that lifestyle. I couldn't walk out and rip off my [head garb] after the first song. It would be disrespectful.

Plus I think religion can be a form of separatism. It keeps people OUT. It's like, we all pray, there's one God, you know what I mean? But that doesn't mean I'm not spiritual.

Where were you on September 11, 2001?

I was on my tour bus from Denver to Canada. I was sleeping, and my manager woke me up. He was like, "You *have* to watch this!" They closed the border to Canada, so we rerouted to Seattle and then LA. I was making crazy calls trying to get through because I know so many people in New York.

> "We have to go bigger, we have to go for peace. If we DON'T come to a bigger, peaceful situation, more people will die."
> —Eve

That weekend I went to Miami just to chill out, but I couldn't relax . . . flying was so difficult. I felt like I was in a different country. It was so scary to see those big men walking around with those guns. And on the flight it made me nervous to think, "I'm on the plane now . . . those people [on September 11] were on the plane . . . did they know? And do they really know how to keep this from happening again?" But what are you going to do, you know?

The whole anthrax thing scared me the most. That was crazy. Right after it started, I got a package delivered to me at my hotel in New York with no return address. So I called my assistant, all, "You have to come open this for me!" and she goes, "I quit!" We laughed. You just have to laugh. You have to find a way to laugh.

How are you feeling about the future these days?

It's weird because, after September 11, it kinda brought everybody together. Black, white, Asian, whatever. It was like nobody was concerned about race anymore. But it took a tragedy for that to happen. I also worry about: Is it gonna stay this way? Or are we gonna go back to race issues, to hating each other?

Do you think we're moving toward peace?

I think we want peace, but we're all riled up. It's like we just wanna punish the people who did this. Which I can understand . . . but the thing is we have to go bigger, we have to go for peace. If we DON'T come to a bigger, peaceful situation, more people will die. Is that good or is that bad?

What can we do? This situation is so huge, a lot of us worry that there's really nothing they can do.

No, you matter. You have influence. Don't forget that parents do listen to their children. Young people do matter.

—**EVE**, a Philadelphia native, has redefined women's roles in hip-hop since bursting onto the scene in 2000 with her first hit, "Love Is Blind," which was an anthem against domestic violence. She's dedicated herself to empowering women, and rocking hard, ever since.

WHAT were you THINKING?

WHAT WERE YOU THINKING when you saw what was happening on September 11, 2001?

Some people were horrified, some of us were confused, some of us didn't believe it, some of us didn't understand how major it all was. What were you thinking? What's the thing *you* remember the most?

The first thought that crossed my mind was, "A month ago I was there! It could have been me!" The truth is I'm still thinking of it.
—Panayiota, 16
Cyprus

I thought of all those people who were stuck at the top of the buildings knowing they weren't going to make it out and talking to their loved ones before they died. My heart is still broken.
—Shannon, 16
Seymour, Connecticut

I cried for all the people who lost their innocence that day, the children, the families, and the world.
—Inisia, 17
Mount Vernon, New York

I didn't understand it, or want to.
—Becky, 13
St. Louis, Missouri

PEACE THEME SONG
"Imagine,"
written by
John Lennon
*You may say
I'm a dreamer,
but I'm not the only one*
—nominated by Susan, 19,
Baltimore, Maryland

I'm Muslim and Palestinian. I felt bad for all the innocents who were killed, and I also thought: They will know how we have suffered.
—Ali, 16
to Alloy.com

My first thought was, "That's it, the world is officially crazy."
—Liat, 17
Jerusalem, Israel

I thought that I was so lucky that it didn't happen here, in my town.
—Debbie, 17
Rochester, New York

All I wanted was to find my little sister. I knew she wasn't in New York or anything, but I needed to see her.
—David, 17
São Paolo, Brazil

Do they feel it when they kill people?
—Shannon, 15
Atlanta, Georgia

I prayed. It's the best way I know to clear my mind when I get pissed off or frustrated at someone or the world. That day in September, I spent the afternoon praying, not really talking to God but more just trying to escape a little, and when everything around me was fear, I found some peace. Nothing made sense, but I knew it would all be okay somehow.
—Elliott, 17
Denver, Colorado

The World Reacts

HORRIFIED CITIZENS in countries around the world looked to their leaders to help make sense of everything that happened on September 11, 2001. Here is what a few of those world leaders had to say.

"We can only imagine the terror and carnage there and the many, many innocent people who have lost their lives. This was perpetrated by fanatics who are utterly indifferent to the sanctity of human life, and we, the democracies of this world, are going to have to come together to fight it and eradicate this evil completely from our world."

—PRIME MINISTER TONY BLAIR OF GREAT BRITAIN

Sept. 21, 2001. Britain's Prince William signs a book of condolences at the U.S. Consulate in Edinburgh, Scotland. The prince, accompanied by his father Prince Charles, signed the book for the families and friends of victims of the Sept. 11, 2001 terror attacks in the United States.

Sept. 23, 2001. In Beijing, a Canadian woman watches as her son prays in front of a bed of white roses during a memorial to honor the victims of the Sept. 11 terrorist attacks on the United States.

"I hurry to express to you and your fellow citizens my profound sorrow and my closeness in prayer for the nation. Those who believe in God know that evil and death do not have the final say."

—POPE JOHN PAUL II

"France is deeply upset to learn of the monstrous attacks that have just struck the United States. In these terrible circumstances, all French people stand by the American people. We express our friendship and solidarity in this tragedy."

—PRESIDENT JACQUES CHIRAC OF FRANCE

"The entire international community should unite in the struggle against terrorism. . . . This is a blatant challenge to humanity."

—PRESIDENT VLADIMIR PUTIN OF RUSSIA

"There can be no doubt that these attacks are deliberate acts of terrorism, carefully planned and coordinated, and as such I condemn them utterly. Terrorism must be fought resolutely wherever it appears."

—UN SECRETARY-GENERAL KOFI ANNAN

"Today the whole world and here in Mexico began with this high-impact news, this criminal act of terrorism, which we reject along with all forms of violence. We reiterate our complete, emphatic rejection of all forms of violence and all forms of terrorism."

—PRESIDENT VICENTE FOX OF MEXICO

"We completely condemn this serious operation. . . . We were completely shocked. . . . It's unbelievable, unbelievable, unbelievable."

—YASSER ARAFAT, PALESTINIAN LEADER

Sept. 13, 2001. Palestinian school girls stand for a moment of silence after the Palestinian flag at their secondary school was lowered to half-staff in Gaza City.

"Irrespective of the conflict with America it is a human duty to show sympathy with the American people, and be with them at these horrifying and awesome events which are bound to awaken human conscience."

—GENERAL MUAMMAR GADHAFI, LIBYA

"None of us will ever forget this day, yet we go forward to defend freedom and all that is good and just in our world."

—PRESIDENT GEORGE BUSH

World News

NEWSPAPERS AROUND THE WORLD were forced to stop the presses for the biggest story in recent years. Although the headlines, of course, appeared in many different languages, the sentiments are clear.

"Pure Evil"
Herald Sun
Sydney, Australia
September 13, 2001

"Apocalipsis"
Razón
La Paz, Bolivia
September 12, 2001

"Thousands Die"
Free Press
Winnipeg, Canada
September 12, 2001

"Monstruoso Ataque"
Segunda
Santiago, Chile
September 11, 2001

"Terrorkrieg: Amerika"
Pforzheimer Zeitung
Berlin, Germany
September 12, 2001

"Atak Na USA"
Zycie Warszawy
Warsaw, Poland
September 12, 2001

"The Mourning After"
The Evening Post
Wellington, New Zealand
September 13, 2001

"Muerte"
El Correo
Madrid, Spain
September 12, 2001

HOW DID YOU HELP OUT AFTER 9-11?

WHILE PEOPLE IN NEW YORK, Washington, D.C., and Pennsylvania tried to pitch in where they could to help dig out from under the rubble and find a way to heal, others around the country struggled to find ways to lend a hand. There are a million stories of teens showing remarkable selflessness, kindness, commitment, and integrity.

Some people got organized and held fund-raisers. Others responded in quieter ways. But there's no question, young people all around the country pitched in after September 11.

Here are some of those stories.

> We all came together in a way that we have not done in a long time. My school has six groups called pods, and my pod, the eighth-grade pod, raised $900 for the relief effort. There are lots of things we can't help with, but there are things we can help with. We need to remember that.
> —Emily, 14
> Denver, Colorado

My youth group had been trying to raise money so that we could have some kind of fun youth activity, and we had been planning a pancake breakfast in September. We went ahead and held the breakfast, but instead of keeping the $150 for ourselves, we donated it to the victims in New York and Washington.
—Ginger, 13
Oklahoma City, Oklahoma

—RUSSIAN

Urbandale High School students in Urbandale, Iowa, reflect during a moment of silence at a pep rally.

Me and my friends are all around 13, so we couldn't give blood, but when the president asked us to mail in money, we totally did that. I mailed in what I had and kept thinking how it might help someone, somewhere. I like that feeling. I'll look for that feeling again.
—Micaela, 13
Kernersville, North Carolina

I'm president of my student council, and by the afternoon of 9/11 I was working with my sponsor to organize a money drive and a blood drive. We raised around $900 and donated over 40 pints of blood. A few weeks after the attacks, we wondered if everyone was ignoring everyone else in the world who needed help, so we organized a food drive for a local homeless organization. Even though we weren't doing things for the 9/11 victims, we knew what we were doing was just as important.
—Danielle, 17
Austin, Texas

The synagogue by my house hosted an interfaith service, which a lot of the people in the neighborhood attended. It really brought us together as a whole, showing that everyone was affected. People brought candles and signs to the promenade, which has a view of the New York skyline, which doesn't look the same.
—Deena, 16
Brooklyn, New York

There's a woman who lives in my building who is an amazing cook, and she spent that whole week making food for the firehouse down the block, which lost eight people. I helped her deliver the stuff. It was scary to see the firemen cry.
—Pat, 19
New York City

Two of my classmates and I decided that we would go to as many funerals as possible for firefighters who were lost in the towers to support the families. We went to six funerals. We kept thinking they were going to get easier, but they didn't.
—Rosario, 16
Queens, New York

A group of my best friends and I, on the day after the attack, thought, "We're old enough to make a difference and help out!" So one sixth-grade teacher agreed that if we raised $12,000, she would shave her head completely. So we stayed after school EVERY day, went to businesses, collected money at lunch, and went door-to-door until about a month and a half later, when we totaled it up. We were a few hundred over our limit. Almost every news channel and the biggest radio station in St. Louis came for the head shaving. It felt great to give back!
—Erica, 14
St. Louis, Missouri

At my school people came up with the idea to bring in sweatshirts and send them up to New York for the firefighters and rescue workers. Each grade brought in a different size (XL, XXL, XXXL), and each person signed their name and grade on a little tag attached to the sweatshirt. After we sent them to New York, the school secretary received a call from a firefighter working at Ground Zero, thanking one of the sixth-grade students, and she also got a call from a firefighter thanking me for the sweatshirt I sent to him.
—Michelle, 13
Hoover, Alabama

A Simple Plan

ASHLEY AND HER THREE SISTERS, Aubrey, 15, Alana, 14, and Alyssa, 10, were extremely lucky on September 11, 2001, when their father, who works in the Pentagon, escaped injury. In response to the tragedy, the girls lined up with their mother to donate blood but were told they were too young.

Determined to contribute somehow, the girls took a neighbor's suggestion and started washing cars for donations. "Just because we're kids doesn't mean we can't try to help our country recover," said Alyssa. Within two weeks they'd held four local car washes and quickly raised thousands of dollars

"When something needs to get done, no matter how impossible it seems, it can be done."

–ASHLEY, 16

ALEXANDRIA, VIRGINIA

The washes weren't an easy thing to pull off. When we asked the girls what the most challenging thing about the events was, they couldn't narrow it down. They had to recruit washers, find locations, make posters and flyers, call local radio stations to get the word out, get supplies, direct traffic, collect money, clean up afterward . . . and keep all the washers full of snacks and lemonade the whole time!

What kept them going? "What we do today will determine the kind of world we live in when we're grown. Plus something happening like this makes us all realize that really, we're in this thing together," explained Aubrey.

Psyched by their success, the girls founded Wash America, a national Internet campaign to encourage people to hold local car washes to raise money. Two of Virginia's members of Congress, Representative Tom Davis and Senator John Warner, got involved,

Ashley, Alyssa, Alana, and Aubrey clean up during a Wash America event.

declaring a series of Wash America weekends, and Frankie Muniz, of *Malcolm in the Middle*, even pitched in at an event in Los Angeles!

"Probably the most rewarding thing was realizing that we are NOT powerless like we used to think. It has blown us away to see how people all over America liked our idea enough to jump on board!" said Alana.

In February 2002, after 80 Wash America events in over 30 states, the girls donated $84,000 to the Red Cross.

Uneasy at Home

"I was appalled. I really couldn't believe that this had happened. . . . Islam doesn't teach people to kill. This was not a jihad. Jihad is not about attacking innocent people."

—RUKHSANA, 16
HOUSTON, TEXAS

RUKHSANA, A MUSLIM STUDENT originally from Tanzania, and Askari, a Muslim student originally from Pakistan, both noticed changes in how they were treated in their school hallways after September 11, 2001. Although neither one was physically harassed or abused, they both were certain that people at school were behaving quite differently.

Instead of keeping their heads down and waiting for tensions to ease up, these two brave students, from different Houston schools, gave long interviews to *The Magnet Tribune* (a paper distributed to several local high schools) in hopes of showing other students that neither they, nor the vast majority of Muslims around the world, agreed with the terrorist attacks on Sptember 11, 2001. Askari followed up with a column in his own high school paper. (See page 88-89.)

But there was more. Both Rukhsana and Askari also wanted to make sure that other students in their area understood the kind of prejudice they, as Muslims, experienced. They were determined to give others a real taste of what they had to deal with in the weeks

سَلَام

—ARABIC

following the attacks—the comments, the glares, the harassment. "Sometimes when I go out, I feel as if people stare at me and think I caused this," said Rukhsana. "[But] my friends stick by my side. Our friendships have gotten stronger."

So how were their interviews received? "My friends were proud [of my column]," said Askari. "Some told me that it was good that I had 'the guts' to write something like that. A few kids in band posted a clipping of it from the newspaper onto the wall in the band hall for others to see. Whether it was helpful or not, I don't really know because later on that week I heard that an Afghani girl was harassed by a student. I'm just glad I wrote the column."

Like thousands of students across the country, Rukhsana and Askari shared their stories to educate the rest of the world about what unique pressures Muslim students face and challenge us to help make things better . . . for everyone.

PEACE THEME SONG
"Joy to the World," performed by Three Dog Night
Joy to the fishes in the deep blue sea
Joy to you and me
—nominated by Itumeleng, 15, Vanderbijlpark, South Africa

"I tried not to take the comments personally, but it's hard to do that when you know those comments aren't directed toward you, but rather all people like you."

—ASKARI, 16
HOUSTON, TEXAS

My Name Has Meaning
By Askari Mohammed

My first name means a warrior or a person of high rank and power in the military; maybe a general. My last name is the most common name in the world today. So my name has meaning. And no one can take that away from me.

I'd always been made fun of ever since I was an innocent child in elementary school. Of course, back then I was made fun of for my ears. Not that they're perfect today, but my ears are no longer a concern to me.

On September 11, when a student yelled out, "Hey! You must be the son of that Bin Laden guy!" and laughed with his buddies down the hall, I gave him credit for that one. It was original, and the first time I had heard a remark like that.

But I expected it. It was a natural response after all, considering the incidents of that morning. I can stand, even ignore an

—Urdu

insult like that. But I cannot tolerate things that have happened to other people.

Why do Muslim girls wearing hijabs have to be harassed? Why do mosques around the world have to be attacked? Why does a car shop in Houston have to be burned down, just because the owner is Pakistani? Why do thousands of men and women have to die in New York and Washington because of some knife-wielding terrorists who hijacked American planes?

Ignorance. Because the man behind the terrorist attacks is just as ignorant as the man who torched the car shop, who is just as ignorant as the student that saw me as the son of a terrorist.

Not being born in America does not make me an apathetic person. Coming from Pakistan does not prohibit me from feeling sorrow for those who lost their lives. I am no different from any other person. I wonder—just like everyone—about what America will do now. I feel—just like everyone—the loss of innocence. And most of all I see—just like everyone—the greatest tragedy America has ever faced.

So they can say I'm not American, that my family is to blame for all that has happened. They can take away my identity because to them I am a terrorist. But I'll just smile, laugh to myself, and think: I'm Askari Mohammad. My name has meaning. And no one can take that away from me.

Rising to the Challenge

WHAT DO YOU DO when you feel like you have nothing to contribute to a national crisis? If you're a musician, like Evan, Raleigh, and their friends in Bend, Oregon, you make music. As soul diva Angie Stone says, "I think that music is healing, and we have no idea what tomorrow holds. When people are speechless, they rely on musicians to come with a relieving message."

We can taste your tears that fall,
we hear you crying
Holding on to freedom's call,
your healing's coming

—"RISE AGAIN, AMERICA," WRITTEN BY EVAN EARWICKER
AND RALEIGH WILLARD

Evan, 16, and his friends Raleigh, Kevin, and Curt, of Mountain View High School in Bend, Oregon, knew they could find a helpful message to share. All four were good musicians, and all four were part of the MVHS choir. Knowing they had holiday concerts right around the corner, they decided to take advantage of the audience they'd be playing for to raise money for the cause.

Evan masterminded the plan to record a benefit CD featuring the MVHS choir performing holiday music on his home sound equipment and sell the CD at their 2001 holiday performances to raise money for victims on the East Coast.

But their crowning achievement was the powerful, show song he and his friends wrote and recorded for the CD, titled "Rise Again, America." On the strength of that song, as well as the other recordings on the CD, the four aspiring rockers were able to raise several thousand dollars for the relief funds.

Rock On

> "They say that people are getting sick of benefit shows, but I think I'd be a heck of a lot more tired of being one of those people who needs help."

—KRISTIN, 21
KANSAS CITY, MISSOURI

KRISTIN IS THE BASSIST for Kansas City rockers Onward Crispin Glover, who with several local bands in Kansas City organized the series of "By Kids, for Kids" concerts to benefit the victims of September 11. Other bands that donated their talents included local bands Flybox, King Suckerman, Thulium, Moaning Lisa, and Corinna Fugate, who brought down the house with her folky tune "Dear America."

The three rock shows, held in November and December 2001, were aimed at giving area teenagers, who could easily afford the $10 ticket price, a way to be a part of the relief efforts in New York and Washington. All of the proceeds were donated to funds established to help victims of the attack. "There's a lot of kids who haven't had a chance to help out yet, and this is an easy opportunity," said Andrea, 17, a concertgoer. The shows also gave area kids a much needed opportunity to let off some steam.

By the end of the year they'd raised several thousand dollars. Rock on!

PEACE THEME SONG
"Dig In,"
written by
Lenny Kravitz
There ain't no time
for you to spare
If you ain't part of
the game then how can
you find a solution
—nominated by Alannah, 18,
Salem, Massachusetts

—WELSH

Freedom's Other Face

When I saw the dead and dying Afghani children on TV, I felt a newly recovered sense of national security. God Bless America.

ON A T-SHIRT WORN BY KATIE, 15
CHARLESTON, WEST VIRGINIA

ON THURSDAY, NOVEMBER 1, 2001, a judge in Charleston, West Virginia, ruled that a 15-year-old student at Sissonville High School could not wear a T-shirt that sarcastically criticized the U.S. bombing in Afghanistan.

Katie, a sophomore, created and wore the T-shirt to class to protest the war on terrorism. School officials also objected to Katie's promotion of a student anarchy club she belongs to, a club that actively opposes war overseas. "I don't want war," said Katie. "I think that what we're doing to them is just as bad as what they did to us, and I think it needs to be stopped."

Katie was frequently verbally and physically harassed at school after wearing her shirt. One student pushed her into a locker. Another wore a retaliatory tee, which read, Go Back Where You Came From, meant to make a point that was lost on Katie, who is from Charleston so has nowhere to "go back" to. Still, Katie felt threatened. School officials, operating under the belief that Katie was creating her own problems and that she represented a threat to the peace and safety of the school, suspended Katie for three days.

"I think it's crazy," Katie said. "Everyone else in that school can say how they feel toward certain things, unless you say something that no one else agrees with. I just don't think that is fair."

Katie, who believed she was being denied her freedom of speech, took her case to court, where she was turned down by the Charleston judge, who ruled that her T-shirt was "inappropriate" and could "disrupt the educational process." Katie appealed the case, but three weeks later the West Virginia Supreme Court upheld the original Charleston ruling.

Katie's mother eventually removed her from the school and opted for home schooling as the harassment increased. Katie stands by her tee and her political beliefs. "I've learned not to give up. It's okay to think differently. It's normal."

Before and After: How Has Your Life Changed?

SEPTEMBER 11 AFFECTED EVERYONE in a different way. Some of us felt like completely different people afterward; some of us were struggling to figure out exactly what has changed. What about you—how has your life changed since the terrorist attacks of September 2001?

My sister is a teacher, and two of her students lost parents in the attack. I realized I should value what I have . . . my parents, my friends, people who love me. I've learned not to take things for granted, but to cherish your surroundings and the people you love.
—Collette, 16
Mountain Lakes, New Jersey

There's no way I ever would have said, before September, that I wanted to join the military. But now I wish I was old enough to sign up.
—James, 15
Denver, Colorado

I've become more accepting of other people and their beliefs. I have also learned that hate will never solve anything.
—Stephanie, 15
Carthage, New York

Before September 11 if you saw a lunch box on the street, you wouldn't think it was a bomb. If you saw sugar on the backseat of a bus, you wouldn't think it was a deadly disease. Now you never know.
—Clarissa, 13
Chicago, Illinois

Now I see that we all know what it's like to live with fear, even Americans. It's like a bad song you can't get out of your head.
—Irena, 16
Valjevo, Serbia

I don't look at some countries as a whole anymore because many people in countries believe that their government is corrupt and evil. I feel sorry for the people in Afghanistan, who have never even made a decision for themselves.
—Courtney, 13
Houston, Texas

I think about the way people live a lot more, including myself. Some people just don't appreciate their lives and do everything possible to ruin them. We all need to learn to live up to our full capabilities, to our full potential, because you never know when tragedy may strike and take everything away. I've thought a lot about what makes someone a good person and what makes someone else a bad person, and I'm still trying to figure it out.
—Cortney, 16
Spartanburg, South Carolina

Here in South Africa, we thought we were living in a safer time [compared to the violent unrest of the 1980s and 1990s], but an event like September 11, a disaster of that magnitude, in the USA, made me realize anything can happen.
—Christopher, 19
Johannesburg, South Africa

Mir
—SERBO-CROAT

There has been no major change in my life, except for, possibly, the greater awareness, appreciation, and love of what we have here in America. I believe I also appreciate more the police officers, firemen, and other emergency-rescue workers who risk their lives every day in small and large situations.

—Jennifer, 18
Franklin, Kentucky

My life is pretty much the same. I did not want to change because of this. I didn't want anyone or any group of people to change things for me.
—Billy, 14
Old Bridge, New Jersey

I used to think that America was the greatest, that everyone in the world wanted to be like us, but now I realize there are many people in the world who absolutely hate us. I don't get it, because I don't hate them.

—Dan, 14
Fort Meyers, Florida

Since 9/11, my life has taken a much more peaceful turn. I have always been a peaceful person, but now I actively try to keep the peace wherever I go. I never hide my feelings anymore. If there is a chance I won't see someone again, and now I know there is always that chance, I make sure they know how I feel. I say "I love you" all the time. I was so proud of the USA and the whole world because we showed such strength and unity.
—Liz, 14
Fort Collins, Colorado

Bake
—BASQUE

To me, it was a shock, but no more drastic than the lives we lose daily in the Middle East.
—Omar, 17
Amman, Jordan

Every time I see an audience on a TV show or a crowd at a game, all I think about is how many people are there and how many would die if that stadium or whatever got hit.
—Kel, 16
San Diego, California

My thoughts were blackened by that horrible day. I see Arab Americans around me now, and sometimes I just wonder. I wonder if they're out to get me and my family and the country I live in. I know that there are only a few bad guys, and I know it's terrible where my mind takes me, and I try to fight against it, but it's true, and it's sad.
—Whitney, 16
Detroit, Michigan

I'm from Bangladesh, not the Middle East, but ever since September 11, people ask me where I'm from, and I can't help feeling they look at me suspiciously. It makes me mad at everyone . . . the hijackers for making people think this way, and everyone who suspects me, for believing everyone with brown skin is a terrorist.
—Ali, 16
New York City

I live near an airport, and every time I hear an airplane in the sky, I watch it. I'm not so sure I'll ever feel comfortable flying again.
—Meghan, 17
Belleville, New Jersey

"Everything was going to be so perfect."

—JONELLE, 18
BRIGHTON, COLORADO

JONELLE AND HER FIANCÉ, JOSHUA, 19, high school sweethearts who'd been dating for a few years, were planning to be married on September 29, 2001. The plan was for a big, traditional wedding, including a white dress, a lavish party, and friends and family from around the country all celebrating together.

But when Joshua, a soldier, was deployed to join Operation Enduring Freedom in the weeks following the terror attacks, their once-in-a-lifetime ceremony was put on hold . . . indefinitely. Jonelle had to hang up her dress for the time being, guests had to change their travel arrangements, and the band had to try and find another gig.

Still, Jonelle, who graduated last year and now lives and works in her hometown of Brighton, Colorado, holds out hope that eventually he'll come home safe, and they'll have the wedding she's dreamed about. But for now, all she can do is wait.

Tens of thousands of military men and women, most of them in their late teens and early twenties, were sent to the Middle East and Central Asia—as well as other hot spots around the world—to face the uncertainty of the War on Terror. They were forced to leave their friends, families, and significant others at home to watch, and worry.

PEACE THEME SONG
"What's Goin' On," performed by Marvin Gaye
You know we've got to find away
To bring some lovin' here today
—nominated by Inisia, 17, Mount Vernon, New York

* * *

"You know how we always say, 'See you later'? One thing I've realized from September 11 is that you can't ever say that for sure. People go to work and don't come back. One minute they're living and the next they're not."

—KOBE BRYANT, LOS ANGELES LAKERS

"I'm very angry. But anger is not a solution. The only solution is to achieve peace. [And] my father said a weapon is not a solution for peace."

—ABDUL MAJEED ARSALA, 16, UNION CITY, CALIFORNIA

MAJEED, A HIGH SCHOOL STUDENT, worries about midterms, loves sports, and bickers with his younger brothers, just like many of us. But Majeed has seen more than his fair share of tragedy.

Majeed's father, Abdul Haq, was an important Afghan anti-Taliban leader for many years and one of the most promising figures in the future government of Afghanistan. After the United States began air strikes in October 2001, the Taliban government captured Haq and publicly hanged him in Kandahar.

This was not the first moment of family horror endured by Majeed. Just two years earlier, in 1999, Majeed saw his mother and youngest brother shot and killed by enemies of his father while they slept in a refugee camp in Pakistan. It was following that tragedy that Majeed moved with his three younger brothers and younger sister to stay with relatives in the United States. His father continued to travel in and around Afghanistan, even though he understood how dangerous it was. The last time Majeed spoke to his dad, Haq was on his way into Afghanistan to meet with other Afghan leaders about overthrowing the Taliban.

"I said, 'Be careful, because the thing that you are going to do is very dangerous.' And then I thought I should get off the phone,

October, 2001. Abdul Majeed Arsala looks at a poster of his father Abdul Haq.

because we kept being interrupted by people trying to talk to my dad. I didn't want to waste his time."

Haq was captured and executed just four days later. All five of his living children are now orphans.

Although he's angry, Majeed hasn't stopped hoping for peace. "I will try my best to follow his footsteps."

Majeed refuses to believe that his father died in vain.

April 11, 1998. A Belfast woman walks with her daughters in a Catholic neighborhood of Belfast.

"For those who say it cannot be done, let us remember that humanity learned to abolish slavery. Our task now is no less than the abolition of violence and war. We can rejoice and celebrate today because we are living in a miraculous time. Everything is changing and everything is possible."

—MAIREAD CORRIGAN
THE VISION OF PEACE

Mairead Corrigan & Betty Williams ◆ Ireland

IN 1974 a car, being driven by an Irish Republican Army fighter who'd just been shot by snipers, slammed into a Belfast sidewalk, killing three kids and critically injuring their mother. Mairead Corrigan, the children's Catholic aunt, and Betty Williams, a Protestant mother in the neighborhood, were among the first at the scene of the crash.

The tragedy brought the two women together, and they committed themselves to ending the cycle of Catholic-versus-Protestant violence that has kept Northern Ireland on edge for centuries. Since 1969 over 50,000 people have been killed or injured in the area as a result of the conflict. Corrigan and Williams founded The Peace People, a coalition group of ordinary Catholics and Protestants

> *"They approached the ordinary men and women of every day with a clear and simple message: we must put an end to the use of violence and to acts of terrorism."*
> —NOBEL PRIZE COMMITTEE, 1976,
> ON THE WORK OF CORRIGAN AND WILLIAMS

dedicated to peace in the region. The women organized and led scores of marches and demonstrations throughout Ireland, Northern Ireland, and England. They reminded the world that many victims are innocent, even children, and that this is as unacceptable as it is horrific.

The two women were awarded the Nobel Peace Prize in 1976. They continue to travel the world, speaking out for peace.

After many years of talks and agreements (including the ground-breaking Good Friday Agreement in 1998; see page 43), fighters in Northern Ireland finally agreed to lay down their arms for good in October 2001.

✳ ✳ ✳

> *"I was most certainly not one of those brave souls who risked their lives for others in the middle of the killing zone. Several civilians were shot for their courageous acts, but thankfully, I was not one of those who lost a family member in the slaughter. I was a scared sixteen-year-old who did everything that he could to stay alive in a situation of utter confusion and carnage."*
> —*Matt Morrison, one of thousands of witnesses to the January 30, 1972, killing of 14 unarmed Catholic protesters by British soldiers in Belfast, Northern Ireland. The event is remembered as Bloody Sunday.*

> *How long?*
> *How long must we sing this song?*
> —"Sunday Bloody Sunday," written by **U2**

Asel Asleh ◆ Israel

"Today I will be asked to choose between what they call 'protecting' and what they call 'forgiving.' Will my choice be the right thing to do, or the wrong thing to do? A friend of mine once said, 'Out beyond ideas of right-doing and wrong-doing, there is a field. I'll meet you there.' Until we meet in the field, my friend . . . take care."

—ASEL ASLEH, 1983–2000

ISRAEL

ASEL ASLEH, a Palestinian peace activist, was only 17 when he was killed in an uprising in Israel on October 2, 2000, while trying to help a wounded friend. Asel, who was an active member of the Seeds of Peace organization and planned to work for peace throughout his life, is remembered most by those who knew him for having an easy laugh and a great sense of humor.

The tragic nature of Asleh's death attracted over 30,000 people to his funeral. Because he was one of the first to die in the latest round of violence, and because he had been so dedicated to building bridges between Jews and Muslims in the region, Asel's life, and tragic death, captured the imagination of his community and the world. Israel, which includes Bethlehem, Jerusalem, Nazareth, and many other holy sites, sits on the crossroads of three worldwide religions (Islam, Christianity, and Judaism) and countless smaller ones (Baha'i, Druze, and others). War has been a reality for the region for thousands of years but has increased drastically since 1948, when Israel declared itself independent. Israeli Jews say they have historical rights to the land; Palestinian Muslims believe the land belongs to them. While most in the area favor peaceful coexistence, radicals on both sides continue to use violence to try to push the other side out of the area.

The latest round of attacks began in September 2000, when Israeli leaders infuriated Palestinian leaders by visiting sacred Islamic ground (a location that also has significance in Jewish history), and Palestinian bombers began retaliating with terrorist acts. The violence snowballed, and Israeli retaliations have been harsh. Dozens of teenagers on both sides, including innocents like Asel and his friend, have been injured or killed, thousands are mourning loved ones, and millions more are deeply involved in the conflict.

✳   ✳   ✳

"I've lived all my life, dreaming to go back to my home-land, Jerusalem. I don't care who is my neighbor, I don't care who is the ruling government, as long as I'm on a land called Jerusalem, Palestine."

—Omar, 17, Amman, Jordan

Omar is a Palestinian refugee whose family was forced to move, over 30 years ago, from their home on what is now the West Bank when Jewish settlers moved in. Like most Palestinians and many others around the world, Omar calls the region Palestine instead of Israel.

✳   ✳   ✳

"We're here, they're here. What's the big deal?"

—Etai, 14, Jerusalem, Israel

Etai is a member of a Jewish family that migrated to Israel with hundreds of thousands of others during the twentieth century to create a Jewish nation, which hadn't existed in the region for thousands of years.

*"When I woke up, I heard my parents crying.
I called to them and my father came over to
hold me. 'They are dead. So many of them.'
I felt the whole world had gone black and that
I was falling down deep into nothing. I wish I
had never woken up. I would rather have slept
away forever."*

—ZHANG HUAJIE, A BEIJING STUDENT WHO HAD RETURNED
HOME FROM WHAT HAD BEEN A RELATIVELY PEACEFUL PROTEST
IN TIANANMEN SQUARE THE NIGHT BEFORE

WANG DAN, ZHANG HUAJIE, and several hundred thousand other student pro-democracy protesters staging a massive sit-in for human rights at Tiananmen Square in Beijing, China, never expected the hard-line communist government to roll in tanks on the night of June 3, 1989. But by the time dawn broke, they and the rest of the world knew that while most people escaped injury, too many of their fellow protesters had been killed—many crushed by tanks after refusing, nonviolently, to leave the area.

"The deepest impression I felt was the enthusiasm for idealism, particularly that of the ordinary people: their concern for the youth and their courage in facing danger . . . Whenever I think of their actions during the movement, I feel proud for them. They are the great people"
—WANG DAN, BEIJING STUDENT PROTESTER, ON THE SUPPORT FOR THE STUDENTS AMONG ORDINARY CITIZENS

The crackdown, which extended to any governmental dissent, continued throughout the summer. Hundreds of people were arrested or detained. Reports of torture and executions ran throughout the countryside. Millions of ordinary citizens supported the student protesters, but Chinese president Deng Xiaoping kept the heat on the protesters, calling them "a rebellious clique" and "the dregs of society."

June, July, and August of that year saw little mercy from the government as the protests and the arrests continued. Estimates of the number of people who died in China in 1989 range from several hundred to several thousand. There has never been an official count, and the Chinese government still refuses to comment.

China remains a human rights hot spot, but as the Chinese economy opens up to the rest of the world, the future looks brighter for broader civil rights. Still, experts believe that China will continue to move slowly on making any changes to their one-party system, a system that allows little opposition and very few personal freedoms.

Cause it would take a lot more hate . . .
To stop the fascination
—"Chinese Democracy," performed by **Guns N' Roses**

Part Four

Peace

Tomorrow

Still we will survive
No matter what
My people just stay alive

— "We Will Survive,"
written by **Nas**

—Korean

Continuing Peace

SO THE QUESTION IS, then, what can we do? If we have at least some freedom to choose the path our lives will take (and in the United States, we have a lot), how can we make choices that will bring us, and the world, closer to a lasting peace?

We know now that we can't wait for anyone else to bring us peace. We can't waste time. We can't pin our hopes on anything, really, except ourselves and each other. If we want peace, we have to work for it together . . . and we'll have to keep working for it forever.

Peace, in all its forms, from inner peace to world peace, sometimes feels more and more rare as history plows forward. Sometimes it feels far away. Sometimes it might be hard to imagine that it could ever exist. But that doesn't keep us from reaching, searching, and praying for peace, and it shouldn't keep us from putting in the hard work for it — from ending poverty to improving communication between cultures to creating cultures of mutual respect and securing civil rights for all people.

And actively caring about each other. Like Fred Durst said in late September 2001, "I care about you being alive, and I want you to care about me being alive. Who knows what the world has to bring in the future?"

We now know that peace isn't something to take for granted, and it isn't something to wait around for. Lasting peace is up to us . . . it's something we must build, something we must create. It takes effort, sacrifice, time, trust, and compromise. It takes energy. It takes hope.

And patience. Most of all, it takes patience.

Peace. We can achieve it, but it'll take some work. Are we ready to do what it takes?

> *We must carry on*
> *When the world lets you down*
> —"I Know A Place," written by **Bob Marley**

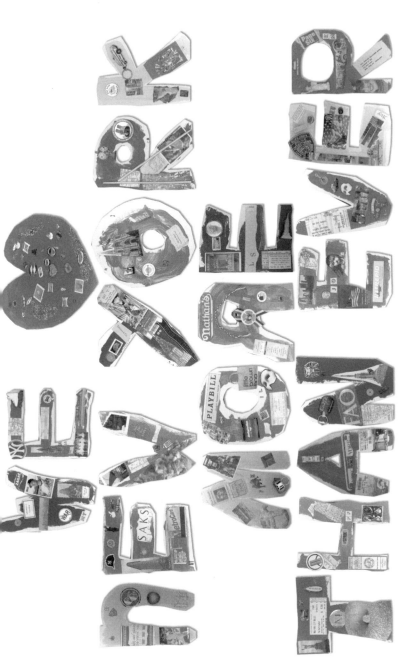

Original art piece, mixed media.

Twenty-one students at Friends Seminary, a private Quaker School in lower Manhattan, created this class art project. Each child painted a single letter on 8 1/2 X 11 inch foam core. The children then collaged bits and pieces of New York City memorabilia on top of their letter, objects ranging from a toy checker cab, a NY license plate, chopsticks, to a ticket to the Nutcracker, even the badge of a student's firefighter uncle who died on 9/11.

IS THIS a
peaceful world?

SOME PEOPLE ARE LUCKY enough to be far removed from acts of violence, while others have to live through them every single day. Do you consider your world, and the world overall, a peaceful one, even as we struggle with violence and terrorism?

No. We always want "revenge, revenge, revenge," to give back to them what they did to us. That's not the way it should be.
—Sasha, 14
Michigan

In the back of my mind, I always know that other people, somewhere, are watching the sky for bombs, starving to death, being forced to fight, watching their babies die. How can I be at peace?
—Darrell, 19
Portland, Oregon

I live in the suburbs and I am pretty sheltered. The only conflict in my life is petty, teenage, high school stuff. But that doesn't mean it's completely peaceful. There's still a lot of prejudice in my school.
—Sarah, 15
Westchester, New York

I think that my world is at peace, at least, my life and the places I go. My family is always peaceful. That's how I want it to be when I have kids.
—Ari, 15
Miami, Florida

My world is not peaceful, because there is war going on in my country, and I am worried about my future.
—Bojan, 16
Ohrid, Macedonia

I believe in myself and my abilities, so my world is very peaceful. Sometimes this peace is shaken, but usually I am happy with what I have and even what I don't have.
—Liat, 17
Jerusalem, Israel

People kill each other every day. For whatever reason, they don't care. The number of peace organizations increases daily, but they still don't meet the number of those groups that are causing terror.
—Omar, 17
Amman, Jordan

There is enough violence in the world, so what I can control, I keep peaceful.
—Billy, 18
Rochester, New York

—ARMENIAN

PEACE THEME SONG
"Winds of Change"
performed by The Scorpions
The future's in the air I can feel it everywhere
—nominated by Rachel, 16, Mercer, Maine

When the planes went down on September 11 and people died, a little bit of everyone in the world died. So did the peace we might have had.
—Kiely, 15
Dublin, Ireland

* * *

I think every person has the ability to effect change. I think we're often led to believe that it's just celebrities who have some ability to effect change, but I think that what's important for us to realize is that every one of us affects the world constantly, through our every smallest action, through our every thought, our every word, the way that we interact with other people.
—ADAM YAUCH, BEASTIE BOYS

PEACE THEME SONG
"War,"
performed by
Edwin Starr
War!
What is it good for?
Absolutely nothing!
—nominated by Elliott, 17,
Denver, Colorado

sìdh
—SCOTS GAELIC

Today's Roots of Conflict

AS LONG AS THERE'S STARVATION, WAR, AND POVERTY IN THE WORLD, it's going to be tough to keep the peace. Need proof? Check out where the world's wars are mostly happening: Africa, the Middle East, Latin America, South Asia. These are also among the poorest places in the world. If we want world peace, we need to pay attention to what's going on around the globe.

- There are, as of 2002, over 60 major armed conflicts going on in the world.

- Children as young as seven years old are currently fighting in civil wars in over 22 countries.

- Over 2 million children and teenagers were killed in armed conflicts around the world from 1990 through 2000. Over 5 million were seriously injured or maimed.

- Over 1 million children and teenagers were orphaned or separated from their families from 1990 through 2000 as a result of war.

- Over 550 million children, about 25 percent of the world's under-18 population, live in "dangerous and unstable" conditions, including extreme poverty or political, racial, or ethnic oppression.

- Over 130 million children worldwide have no access to education at all.

- Over 180 million children and teenagers worldwide suffer from malnutrition.

- Over 250 million children and teenagers worldwide hold down full-time jobs. Many of these are involved in hazardous or exploitative work, including mining, garment work, agriculture, and military service.

*Source: UNICEF, World Health Organization

Daw Aung San Suu Kyi ◆ Myanmar

"Peace is life itself, because a life without peace is hardly a life worth living. But by peace I do not mean a life of passivity, I do not mean a life without action because sometimes we have to act a lot to bring about peace. . . .
We cannot drift along in any imaginary world. There will have to be great sacrifices, tremendous hard work and effort."

—DAW AUNG SAN SUU KYI
YANGON, MYANMAR, 1999

IN 1991 THE NOBEL PRIZE COMMITTEE awarded its annual Peace Prize to Daw Aung San Suu Kyi, a nonviolent resistance leader from the Southeast Asian country of Myanmar (formerly called Burma). She was unable to attend the ceremony because the military government

"Suu is one of those rare individuals who symbolize not just the courage of human beings, but the courage of an entire country. There's an almost mystical identity between her and the Burmese people."
—DAVID ARNOTT, BURMA PEACE FOUNDATION

refused to let her leave the country, a punishment she received for leading several demonstrations in favor of democracy and freedom.

Myanmar, a nation of over 60 million people, is ruled by a military coalition that gives almost no freedoms to its citizens, depriving them of the right to vote, travel freely, or exercise free speech. People there are not guaranteed education, health care, or civil protections under the law. The country is the world's top producer of opium, from which heroin and some methamphetamines are made, and it is widely understood that the government does not crack down on drug trafficking, leading many to believe it depends on the drugs for its money.

Daw Aung San Suu Kyi, daughter of a popular Burmese resistance leader who was gunned down when she was only two, has dedicated her life to keeping her father's hopes for freedom alive. In August 1988 she sparked the watershed 8-8-88 uprising in which millions of people across the country marched against the military, who had taken over the government and nullified election results. The movement lasted for almost two years. Daw Aung San Suu Kyi traveled around her country, speaking for democracy—until military leaders placed her under house arrest, stifling her voice.

But they weren't able to stifle her spirit. Daw Aung San Suu Kyi and her peaceful vision for the future of Myanmar are considered a threat to the security of the military government, which controls its people through terror and intimidation. Although she was freed from house arrest in May 2002, the government continues to monitor her movements and restrict her freedoms.

The Dalai Lama ◆ Tibet

"Peace, in the sense of absence of war, is of little value to someone who is dying of hunger or cold. Peace can only last where human rights are respected, where people are fed, and where individuals and nations are free."

—Tenzin Gyatso, the fourteenth Dalai Lama

The spiritual leader of Tibet, or Dalai Lama, is traditionally identified and selected by Tibetan Buddhist monks when he is very young, in the belief that he is the reincarnation of all the previous Dalai Lamas. The current Dalai Lama, the fourteenth, was discovered at age three by Tibetan Buddhist leaders, who responded to a number of spiritual signs and visions to find the toddler and tested him to make

"Take into account that great love and great achievements involve great risk."

—TENZIN GYATSO

sure that he was the new Dalai Lama. Taken from his family to a monastery in the mountains, the current Dalai Lama spent his childhood and teen years being trained in spiritual and governmental matters to prepare for his destiny of governing Tibet.

But in 1959, when he was 24 years old, Chinese troops occupied his homeland and put it under Chinese rule. Many local leaders were massacred or driven out. The Dalai Lama escaped but has never been allowed to return home.

Even while it remains under Chinese occupation, Tibet has a rich and distinct culture. Ethnically, linguistically, and historically, Tibetans are a separate people, but the Chinese see the area as strategically important for China's future, and the government in Beijing keeps tight control of the region.

A deeply religious Buddhist culture, Tibetans lost their freedom to worship freely, practice cultural traditions, or govern themselves when the Chinese army occupied the land. The Dalai Lama, whose title means, "Ocean of Wisdom," now lives in exile across the border in India. Since his exile, he has dedicated his life to finding a peaceful way to return Tibet to Tibetan rule. In this pursuit he's bravely traveled the world, meeting leaders from many nations and educating the world about the situation in his homeland. He was awarded the Nobel Peace Prize in 1989.

✳ ✳ ✳

"We have a lot to gain from the Tibetans. There are certain lessons that are within Tibetan culture . . . compassion and nonviolence . . . that we really lack in our society."

—ADAM YAUCH, BEASTIE BOYS

Rigoberta Menchú Tum ◆ Guatemala

"Our lives are no longer our own; they can take them away any time."

—RIGOBERTA MENCHÚ TUM, MAYAN REFUGEE

FOR OVER 500 YEARS, ever since Christopher Columbus first planted the Spanish flag in the New World, the indigenous people of the Americas have had their land occupied by violent force and systematically removed from their control.

In many nations, including the United States, Native Americans were massacred and forced onto reserved areas, usually parcels of land with very little value. In many countries indigenous Americans still have very few rights; government and education are often reserved only for people of European descent.

"Rigoberta Menchú grew up in poverty, in a family which has undergone the most brutal suppression and persecution. In her social and political work, she has always borne in mind that the long-term objective of the struggle is peace."
—NOBEL PRIZE COMMITTEE, 1992

The Maya, an ancient American civilization as advanced as that of medieval Europe, was virtually destroyed in the sixteenth and seventeenth centuries by Spanish colonists but still has millions of descendants in Mexico and Central America. Rigoberta Menchú Tum is one of them.

Menchú Tum grew up in a Guatemalan refugee camp set up for the Maya when they were forced to turn over their homes to the Spanish-speaking ruling class. Throughout the 1980s, while she was only in her twenties, she organized dozens of protests against the government, even distancing herself from others fighting for the same cause whose methods she considered too violent. Said Menchú Tum, "We must create a culture of peace. You don't need to have war first to get peace. Instead it should be part of our education, our values. It should be part of our approach to resolving problems. And young people must contribute."

Menchú Tum, now 43 years old, continues to inspire Mayan resistance from Mexico, where she lives in exile. She was awarded the Nobel Peace Prize in 1992.

There's something here I find hard to ignore
There's something that I've never seen before
— *"Flowers of Guatemala,"* written by **R.E.M.**

Jody Williams ◆ International

"It's breathtaking what you can do when you set a goal and put all your energy into it. I think you have to believe you're right. You say, 'This is what we're going to achieve, and this is how we're going to do it.' And if people get upset about it, tough."

—JODY WILLIAMS

DURING THE 1990S, JODY WILLIAMS, a former teacher from Vermont who witnessed the horrors of land mines during her work as a medical volunteer in Central America, started and led the International Campaign to Ban Landmines (ICBL), which gathered speedy support

"The more expeditiously we can end this plague on earth caused by the land mine, the more readily can we set about the constructive tasks to which so many give their hand in the cause of humanity."
—PRINCESS DIANA

around the world. By traveling hard for six straight years and enlisting the help of Princess Diana and other high-profile supporters, Williams persuaded 141 nations, including South Africa, Great Britain, France, Brazil, and Nigeria, to ratify the International Mine Ban Treaty, promising not to produce or use land mines. (The United States is one of the few countries in the world, along with Iraq, Libya, and Russia, that hasn't signed it.) In 1997 Jody Williams was awarded the Nobel Peace Prize.

Every year more than 25,000 civilians die or lose arms or legs by accidentally setting off land mines. Most are in Afghanistan, where dozens of people are hurt or killed every week. The rest are in Ethiopia, Angola, Cambodia, Kosovo, Laos, Croatia, Congo, Sri Lanka, and over 20 other countries. Most are in places that are no longer at war, which means most land mine injuries happen just because an innocent person unknowingly stepped in the wrong spot. As Williams explains, "The land mine cannot tell the difference between a soldier or a civilian—a woman, a child, a grandmother going out to collect firewood to make the family meal. . . . Once peace is declared the land mine does not recognize that peace. The land mine is eternally prepared to take victims. The war ends, the land mine goes on killing."

A huge percentage of land mine victims are children or teens. Too often, these victims weren't even alive during the war when the mines were planted.

*Our seeds will grow
All we need is dedication*
—from "Everything Is Everything," written by **Lauryn Hill**

future peace

No one can see into the future, and while most of us hope for a peaceful world, how realistic is it to believe that we'll truly solve problems of violence, poverty, and hate anytime soon? What do you think? Will the world in the future be more or less peaceful than it is today?

I'm not sure if the future will be more or less peaceful, but I do know that whatever my answer would be, it would have been different on September 10, 2001.
—Maryam, 17
New York City

I think as the years roll by, the world will learn to work together and become more peaceful. That's how history has shown itself to me.
—Cathy, 16
Lansdale, Pennsylvania

If we continue in the way we act now, the future will be much worse.
—Panayiota, 16
Cyprus

I am a human being, and I feel a connection with all humans. As long as another human is being aimed at as a target, then I am being aimed at as a target.
—Shannon, 17
Zionsville, Indiana

Whether or not my life will be peaceful is in God's hands.
—Walter, 17
Sasolburg, South Africa

There will always be fights as long as there are differences in opinion. Sometimes that's good . . . how boring would it be if everyone thought the same? The thing we want is to fight our conflicts in a less violent manner.
—Sarah, 15
Westchester, New York

There is no way to tell, but I believe it will not get any better.
—Mat, 17
Rochester, New York

I hope my life will be a balanced one, with mostly peace but some chaos, without which I wouldn't be able to truly appreciate peace.
—Jacqui, 17
Melbourne, Australia

My life will not be peaceful. I joined the marines to put my life up to make sure 9/11 will never happen again. I do this for others to be safe, so that others may feel peace, even if I don't.
—Carol, 18
Sacramento, California

Pokój

—POLISH

PEACE THEME SONG

"Peace Train,"
written by
Cat Stevens
Oh, I've been smilin' lately,
Dreamin' about the world
as one
—nominated by Dan, 18,
Indianapolis, Indiana

increasing the peace

IT'S ONE THING TO WISH FOR WORLD PEACE. But it's another thing to get up off the couch and do something constructive about it. We all know we'll never get anywhere if we don't have everyone working for peace . . . so how are you making a difference now, and how will you contribute in the future?

My future plans have changed. I no longer think of living in that huge mansion with tons of money and a laid-back job, but instead in a foreign country like Afghanistan, helping other people and giving the money I could spend on luxuries to those who need it more. Why throw around money when someone needs it to stay alive?
—Marcie, 14
Dial, Texas

I'll go out and tell the world how I feel and make sure that I'm heard because every voice matters.
—Sarah, 16
Williamsburg, Virginia

I will always believe the enemy has a face.
—Raya, 14
Jordan

I want to be a journalist, to show the truth and spread knowledge so that maybe people can learn not to repeat the past.
—Inisia, 17
Mount Vernon, New York

By playing sports. It puts us all on the same playing field.
—Omar, 17
Amman, Jordan

I do believe that my life will be a peaceful one. In order to make sure that it will, I plan on joining the FBI and helping out in making America safer than it already is.
—Courtney, 13
Houston, Texas

We must all, everyone, everywhere in the world, consider ourselves one nation.
—Daniel, 17
Vredeport, South Africa

Participate in a peaceful protest for stopping wars and ending suffering.
—Bojan, 16
Ohrid, Macedonia

Happy people provide a peaceful society. I'll try to make people happy as much as I can.
—Burcu, 15
Istanbul, Turkey

Something I've learned is that peace is totally infectious. If you set a good example, people follow it. I am involved with lots of different charities in my community, and I am working on being president of the United States someday. Peace isn't such a far-fetched idea. . . . This world is what we make it, and we can make it great for everyone.
—Liz, 14
Fort Collins, Colorado

—TURKISH

Choose love, not hate. Let the terrorists and the haters be the ones who are wrong. Treat everyone like family regardless of race or religion. We as humans can turn over a new leaf.
—spooky9, to Alloy.com

I love people, not colors, genders, sizes, religions, etc. I will always turn the other cheek. I will work hard to control my temper. This is where I will start.
—Simon, 17
Melbourne, Australia

It's cheesy, but the Golden Rule, "Do unto others as you would have them do unto you," just seems like the simplest solution.
—Carla, 18
Montreal, Canada

The only way for us to ever achieve world peace is if we can make peace with the people around us. Our parents, brothers and sisters, friends, classmates . . .If we can achieve peace in our own world, we can achieve peace in the whole world.
—Jennifer, 18
Franklin, Kentucky

"We need to have courage. We must rely on each other to overcome obstacles and to overcome evil. It's important to have hope."
—ELIJAH WOOD

Delivering Peace

WHEN PRESIDENT KENNEDY was inaugurated in January 1961, one of the first plans he set in motion was the establishment of the U.S. Peace Corps. He envisioned young Americans traveling to distant, destitute

President Kennedy greets college students.

parts of the world not only to help out building homes and providing health care, but to educate people in technology, agricultural techniques, science, and more. His belief was that with the right support, areas in crisis could learn how to improve their situations themselves and create their own opportunities in the world, which is a much more lasting solution to the poverty they faced than just relying on financial assistance from other nations.

The first year volunteers were sent to Ghana, Tanzania, Colombia, the Philippines, Chile, and St. Lucia. Within five years over 15,000 volunteers were in the field, from Afghanistan to China to Jordan to Zambia.

The Peace Corps is still going strong, still committed to making sure it sends the best-possible people overseas. There is a grueling,

A Peace Corps Volunteer shares a greeting and a smile with a mother and child in Ghana.

"And so, my fellow Americans: ask not what your country can do for you—ask what you can do for your country. My fellow citizens of the world: ask not what America will do for you, but what together we can do for freedom."

—JOHN F. KENNEDY
THIRTY-FIFTH PRESIDENT OF THE UNITED STATES
AND FOUNDER OF THE PEACE CORPS

intense application and testing process, and volunteers are trained extensively in the language of the country they are assigned to. It's a two-year commitment, and the work isn't always easy . . . volunteers do everything from digging ditches to teaching English to helping small businesses get started. But it's certainly one of the most amazing and fulfilling experiences available anywhere.

Host country nationals and this Peace Corps Volunteer work together to improve the environment.

"The time of day I look forward to most is building my morning fire. It is my time of epiphany. As I feel the warmth that my own hands created, a fire that pushes back the cold and the dark, replacing them with warmth and light, I know I will live another day. Such an experience defines what it means to be a Peace Corps volunteer."

—MATTHEW HELLER (PEACE CORPS VOLUNTEER, MONGOLIA, 1995–97)

Peace Corps Volunteers and a host country national converse while riding the bus.

> "My parents, who had served as volunteers in Kenya 25 years before I joined the Peace Corps, had absolutely no idea how much influence they had during their two years of service. They did not consider themselves exceptional volunteers; they simply went to class, taught a variety of subjects in the best way they knew how, and loved the people they lived among. But returning with me to their village so many years later, they were struck by the undeniable realization that they had indeed changed people's lives."
>
> — TARA ELIZABETH BEVERWYK (PEACE CORPS VOLUNTEER, MALAWI, 1995–98)

A Peace Corps Volunteer interacts with host country nationals in Belize.

Teaching Peace

SOMETIMES YOU NEED TO GET PEOPLE AWAY from the scene of the conflict if you want to get them to really talk to each other. That's the idea behind Seeds of Peace, which began in 1993 as a summer camp for Palestinian and Israeli teens and has become an international movement dedicated to building trust among young people in war-torn areas of the world.

The Seeds of Peace camp in Maine focuses on creating an international summertime gathering of teens on opposite sites of conflicts (Pakistanis and Indians, Greeks and Turks, Serbs and Croatians, Israelis and Palestinians—including Asel Asleh, page 104) to build lasting understanding, and even friendships, across conflict lines. Throw some American teens into the mix (because the camp is in the United States, and because Americans founded the organization) and the campers have a whole lot of different perspectives, and a whole lot to learn about each other. After a summer of getting to know each other and listening to each other's points of view, the campers maintain their relationships over the year by e-mail.

The hope is that bringing together traditional enemies when they're young will lead to a greater peace when they become the decision makers. It's a long-term investment in a long-term peace.

✳   ✳   ✳

"When I attended the Seeds of Peace camp, I met a boy. It's not important where he's from. What's important is my memory of him, telling the story of his pain, the effect war has had on his family, leaning forward, his thin body, his huge eyes angry and sad. I want people to hear his voice. He should not be so thin, so scared, so angry. He should laugh and run and sing and dream. His 'enemies' should have this freedom as well. War takes away his freedom, it takes away his joy. Every day, I see his eyes in my mind, and he's telling me, 'Maybe I am lost—maybe I will never have peace, but I want to be the last one. I want to be the last one to live with this.'"

—*RACHEL, 16 MERCER, MAINE, SEEDS OF PEACE CAMPER*

We, Seeds of Peace,
young people representing
22 war-ravaged nations,
hereby declare that we are
tired of hatred, violence,
and terror.
—SEEDS OF PEACE CHARTER

Weaving a Web of Peace

DEDICATED TO THE PURSUIT OF PEACE well before September 11, 2001, Billy, an 18-year-old Rochester, New York, high school senior, started TeenWebOnline (http://www.twonline.cjb.net) early in his high school career. It's a site where teens gather to discuss topics like racism, violence, discrimination, and other issues students across the country struggle with every day.

The site, which attracts 10,000 visitors monthly, includes articles and essays by high school students, news on topics that affect teens, facts about violence, interviews with victims, celebrity quotes, ideas for resolving conflicts without resorting to violence, and more. There are links to organizations where teens can get involved.

The site also reaches out to people who think they may be a victim, or a perpetrator, of violence, offering to hook them up with advice and help. Billy's been able to direct dozens of teens to resources closer to their own homes.

> ## "If we don't take action now, then what will our future be like?"
> —BILLY, 18
> ROCHESTER, NEW YORK

Why the Internet? "Millions and millions of people log on to the Internet every day. Using the Internet for a project like mine allows many teens to get involved with each other more easily," Billy explains.

In early 2002 Billy raised funds and flew two survivors of the 1999 Columbine tragedy to schools in his area to talk about their experiences and to inspire kids to stay away from violence, an event he hopes to repeat in the future.

Billy's goal? A future that he has a part in shaping. "What will life be like if we go around not caring about what happens in our society? We need to value each other as human beings and take a stand always, no matter what the situation. Young people have a much larger role than some adults believe. In the decades to come we will be leaders, doctors, teachers, etc. In essence the young people of today are the only ones who can ensure peace in the future."

—GERMAN

Peace Out

SO WHERE ARE WE, ANYWAY?

Are we stuck in a world of war, a never-ending cycle of violence and delicate peace? Or are things not quite that dire?

No matter how bad things get, we all have the power, when faced with any kind of choice, to choose the more peaceful route. We can curb our road rage and not flip off that guy who just cut us off. We can try to understand, and fight against, feelings of prejudice within ourselves. We can commit to join a peace organization and work to resolve specific conflicts around the world or right at home.

The most important choice we get to make is what to believe. We can be optimistic, to know that we can make our points without hurting each other. We can believe that everyone has the right to live and learn and love and make a better life for themselves and that no one is more entitled to those things than anyone else. We can choose to make the first move toward peace rather than waiting for someone else to do it.

If we turn these choices into habits, who knows how far we can move the world?

It's true when they say we are the future. What they mean is that one of these days, we'll be taking over this planet, and it's up to us to create the more peaceful world we want to live in.

Starting right now.

PEACE

Make It Happen!

IT'S ONE THING TO TALK ABOUT WORLD PEACE. But the question is, what are we doing about it? Good news! You, too, can increase the peace! Check out these organizations, just for starters. Get involved, learn more, and participate in the future of peace.

Save the Children

www.savethechildren.org

A nongovernmental group whose mission is to bring food, shelter, medicine, and other necessary supplies to poverty-stricken children and teenagers worldwide.

Seeds of Peace

www.seedsofpeace.org

An organization dedicated to bringing together teens from both sides of war zones as well as teens from the United States in an attempt to create lasting, personal connections among traditional enemies.

UNICEF (United Nations International Children's Emergency Fund)

www.unicef.org

A branch of the United Nations focused on meeting the needs of children afflicted by poverty, war, and crisis around the world. The current UNICEF celebrity ambassadors include Angelina Jolie, Christy Turlington, and Susan Sarandon.

International Youth Cooperation

www.iyoco.org

Their tag line is "Striving for a Peaceful Century." This organization brings together young people from nations around the world to present their concerns to national and international leaders.

Do Something

www.dosomething.org

Do Something donates money to local causes, from cleaning up the environment to tutoring younger students. If you have a great idea, apply to Do Something for money, and they may help you out.

Amnesty International
www.amnesty.org

Dedicated to human rights worldwide, Amnesty International focuses mostly on obtaining freedom for people being held as political prisoners or hostages.

Peace Corps
www.peacecorps.org

The Peace Corps sends young people around the world to help out communities struggling with poverty, war, and other crises. Visit the site to see first-person stories from people who've participated and learn how to get involved.

Human Rights Watch
www.hrw.org

Provides updates on human rights issues around the world.

AFS (American Field Service)
www.afs.org

An international exchange organization that places students and teachers in other countries to live and study and increase peace.

Waging Peace
www.wagingpeace.org

Dedicated to ridding the world of any nuclear threat by lobbying political leaders in countries around the world.

Peace Jam
www.PeaceJam.org

Provides news and information about peace around the world, with a special focus on Nobel Peace Prize winners.

Teen Web Online

http://www.twonline.cjb.net

By teens for teens. Includes news from around the world, celebrity interviews, and ways to keep the peace in your own community.

TakingITGlobal

www.takingitglobal.org

Allows visitors to connect with other students from every country on the planet (almost) and talk about peace, politics, life, music, and how to make the future a better place.

Shine

www.shine.org

A teen-generated, teen-organized website that focuses on issues of race, gender, equality, and nonviolence. Read what others are going through in other American high schools.

International Campaign to Ban Landmines

www.icbl.org

Provides news and information on the struggle to rid the world of land mines.

Nobel Peace Prize

www.nobel.se/peace

Features news and history about the Nobel Peace Prize.

Peace Action

www.peace-action.org

Focuses on news and information about nuclear disarmament and conventional weapon reductions.

Find Out More

Intrigued by some of the great peace leaders profiled in this book? Sink your teeth into these biographies:

MOHANDAS GANDHI
Gandhi, the Man, by Eknath Easwaran (Nilgiri Press, 1997)

MARTIN LUTHER KING, JR.
The Autobiography of Martin Luther King, Jr., by Martin Luther King, Jr., and Clayborne Carson (Warner Books, 2001)

STEVEN BIKO
Biko, by Donald Woods (Henry Holt, 1987)

NELSON MANDELA
Long Walk to Freedom, by Nelson Mandela (Little, Brown, 1995)

MAIREAD CORRIGAN AND BETTY WILLIAMS
Mairead Corrigan and Betty Williams: Making Peace in Northern Ireland (Women Changing the World), by Sarah Buscher, et al. (Feminist Press, 1999)

DAW AUNG SAN SUU KYI
Burma: The Curse of Independence, by Shelby Tucker (Pluto Press, 2001)

THE DALAI LAMA
Freedom in Exile: The Autobiography of the Dalai Lama, by the Dalai Lama (HarperCollins, 1991)

JODY WILLIAMS
After the Guns Fall Silent: The Enduring Legacy of Landmines, by Shawn Roberts and Jody Williams (Oxfam, 1995)

THE NOBEL PEACE PRIZE
Peacemakers : Winners of the Nobel Peace Prize, by Ann T. Keene (Oxford University Press, 1998)

Photo Credits